NO MERCY, NO LENIENCY

By the same author:

The Beaulieu River Goes to War
Beaulieu: The Finishing School for Secret Agents

Co-Author:

The Polygraph Test: Lies, Truth & Science

NO MERCY, NO LENIENCY

COMMUNIST MISTREATMENT OF BRITISH PRISONERS OF WAR IN KOREA

by

CYRIL CUNNINGHAM

WITH A FOREWORD BY
M. R. D. FOOT

LEO COOPER

First published in Great Britain 2000 by
Leo Cooper
an imprint of Pen & Sword Books
47 Church Street
Barnsley
South Yorkshire
S70 2AS

ISBN 0 85052 767 8

A catalogue record for this book is available from the British Library

Typeset in 10/13pt Sabon by
Phoenix Typesetting, Ilkley, West Yorkshire

Printed in England by Redwood Books, Trowbridge, Wiltshire

DEDICATION

To my tutors and mentors in the Intelligence Corps
Major 'John' Young of A.I.9
Major Cyril Hay of M.I.19
Major Gordon Instone I.S.9 (T.A.)

CONTENTS

FOREWORD

BY

M. R. D. FOOT

All things change; even what the old officer class used to regard as something as fixed as the laws of the Medes and Persians, how one ought to
behave if one had the bad luck to become a prisoner of war. One gave
one's name, one's rank, one's number and no other information of any
kind; one's duty was to escape and, failing a successful escape, one did
one's best to make life awkward for the enemy.

Since the end of the wars against Hitler and Hirohito, things have not
looked quite the same. In this book Cyril Cunningham explains, from
inside knowledge, how badly the old rules applied as soon as five years
later, during the war in Korea. Escape there was made much more difficult for British or American fighting men – as it had been in the war
against Hirohito's Japan – by the brute fact that they looked entirely
unlike the local inhabitants through whose villages they might have to
pass. Escapers stuck out like sore thumbs. Besides, they could not look
for that help from passing strangers which had saved so many hundreds
of escapers and evaders in Nazi-occupied Europe; in communist-
dominated North Korea the party and its police ruled with an iron grip.
No one, it seems, managed a complete get-away, though several got out
of their unspeakable camps for some days on end, only to be beaten up
on recapture.

Moreover, within the camps, sticking to name, rank and number only
made trouble. The North Koreans, when they bothered to keep any
prisoners alive (they shot a great many sooner than bother to feed and
shelter them) did not handle them gently; most were consigned to caves
and death from starvation and neglect, or to slave labour gangs that were
worked to death.

The Chinese took a gentler line with their prisoners, but were much
more thorough. Every single man received a prolonged, personal cross-
questioning, often preceded by filling in a long form; nobody found it

feasible even to try to stick to name, rank and number. Chinese initial ignorance of the ways of the west led to some Royal Marines (the first British military p.o.w. they captured) to be taken to task and beaten for their impertinence when they claimed to own motor cycles or motor cars, and yet not a single pig or chicken; a barbarity they soon discovered and not repeated later. None of the prisoners had received any preparatory warning about how much it would, and how much it would not, be safe to vouchsafe to an enemy: an important lacuna in training in how to behave after capture, which has presumably by now long been remedied. Many prisoners had the common sense to keep to themselves what they knew about their fellow prisoners, but they were at the mercy of others who for political or selfish reasons sought to curry favour with their captors by splitting on their comrades in arms.

A surprisingly high proportion of the captured Royal Marines seemed ready to embrace the communist social system and its propaganda, but very few of them were still inclined to the left after repatriation. They received a frosty reception when they called at the CPGB headquarters in King Street and were disillusioned by the poor calibre of the party members they made contact with in their home towns.

It has for years been taken for granted by the news media that the intensely political treatment the prisoners received in captivity led to their having been 'brainwashed'; a myth Mr. Cunningham is at pains to dispel, hardly before time. It is a relief to get the truth established; he leaves room for little doubt.

Mr Cunningham wields a clear pen as well as an informed mind. He is much more interested in the political realities of these men's experiences than in cataloguing their physical sufferings, and explains neatly how they fitted into the cold war propaganda that was being ladled out by the Chinese and North Korean governments as well as by the Russians. Elderly readers will recall, for instance, the allegations that the Americans had used germ warfare in Korea; wholly unsubstantiated in fact yet supported by the confessions of captured American aircrew who had been psychologically harried and physically abused until they agreed to sign.

Studies of human kind under pressure are always interesting; this is a most readable addition to the already extensive literature that bears on this tense and difficult subject.

PREFACE

In this book I have attempted to give a straightforward and integrated account of the treatment of British prisoners of war by the Chinese Communists and the North Koreans during the war with the United Nations Forces in Korea (June 1950-July 1953). Although several books have been published by former p.o.w., these were essentially the personal experiences of a select minority. Nothing has been published by former p.o.w. who collaborated with their captors. The Ministry of Defence Blue Book (actually a pamphlet of 41 pages) on "The Treatment of British Prisoners of War in Korea", which I had a hand in preparing, was published in 1955 but gives no insight into their side of the story. It received a hostile reception from the British press which accused the Government of suppressing information about the behaviour of British officers in captivity. This extreme scepticism arose from the fact that the Blue Book implied that all the so-called 'progressives' among the British prisoners were 'Other Ranks' whereas the Americans had admitted that many of their officers as well as enlisted men had co-operated with the enemy. How was it, the angry press demanded, that British officers alone appeared to be immune to Communist blandishments? That question was never answered and to this day nobody has vouched for the authenticity of the facts in the Blue Book.

Clearly, an overall picture of the treatment of all segments of the prisoner population and the events which occurred in each of the twelve camps in which they were incarcerated can only be given by one who was at the centre of prisoner of war intelligence at the material time.

Soon after the outbreak of the Korean War a defunct Prisoner of War Intelligence organization, M.I.9, was reactivated, renamed A.I.9 and placed under the Air Ministry because it was housed in Air Ministry premises. It's purpose was to collect intelligence on prisoners of war and to teach combat units Conduct After Capture, especially survival techniques.

At that time I was a young, recently qualified Occupational

Psychologist working in Science 4, the Psychology Section of the Department of the Scientific Advisor to the Air Ministry. Before qualifying as a psychologist and before my World War II service in the RNVR I had read law at Cambridge under a truly great authority on Jurisprudence, Professor P.H. Winfield, knowledge which became of inestimable value later, in my Intelligence work. My routine duties at the Air Ministry centred upon validating the selection tests and interview results of RAF apprentices and boy entrants by comparing them with their training outcomes, a job I hated because it involved tabulating masses of data by hand and, using a primitive mechanical calculator, subjecting it to endless, complex statistical calculations that today would be done in a flash by a computer. As a relief from statistical misery I had ventured into some unauthorized research into perceptual deceptions used in World War II camouflage techniques and I also produced a paper on the effects of stealthy interrogation techniques used by the Germans on captured Allied aircrew.

My camouflage interests led to me being sent on a course at Netheravon in Wiltshire where, together with a few senior RAF officers, I not only learned the fundamentals of camouflage and photographic interpretation but was also introduced to the whole business of decoys and deception plans. Thus was I initiated into the world of Intelligence.

Soon afterwards my researches into the effects of stealthy German interrogation techniques came to the notice of the Deputy Director of Security Intelligence of the RAF and, in November 1952, at the age of twenty-six, I was called to an interview by a panel of officers from each of the three services, a group which, unbeknown to me at the time, comprised the senior officers of A.I.9. They wanted to know how I had obtained information that was supposedly highly classified. I told them that I had obtained some of it while still an undergraduate, during a brief stint in one vacation with the RNVR at an air station in Cornwall, but that most of it had come from the Holborn Public Library. The chairman of the panel, Wing Commander 'Jim' Marshall, a well known escaper from the German Stalags, chortled and said that if I was that good at finding and piecing information together I had better come and work for him.

A month or so later I found myself seconded to A.I.9 to conduct research into Communist interrogation and indoctrination methods, with terms of reference handed down to me by an august body, the Joint Intelligence Committee. It was a task which was to tax my knowledge of cognitive psychology and jurisprudence to the limit; the latter proved to be essential for spotting the dirty legal tricks used by the Communists in their 'show' trials.

I was unaware that my hasty secondment was due to the alarm in military circles at the unprecedented behaviour of the British troops held captive by the Communists in Korea. When, eventually, the camps in which they were being held were located by aerial reconnaissance, it was discovered that they were ordinary Korean villages near the Yalu River, the frontier with Communist China, and none of them was fenced with the usual static defences of barbed wire and watchtowers. There appeared to be nothing preventing the prisoners from escaping en masse, and yet nobody had escaped despite having been briefed before going into action that it was their duty to do so if captured. According to a deluge of Communist propaganda, they had no reason to escape since they were being exceptionally well treated. The War Office was outraged by the large numbers of prisoners participating in political rallies within their camps condemning the United Nations aggression and demanding peace on Communist terms! Hence the motive for recruiting a psychologist to look into the enemy's indoctrination methods and their effectiveness. Mercifully the term "Brainwashing" had not yet been invented.

My research into the treatment of British p.o.w. in Korea was a small but significant part of a much larger, gruesome, study. However, the unique political and sociological nature of the treatment impelled the serving officers of A.I.9 to look to me for guidance on all manner of issues and compelled me to spend much time assisting them to collect data and helping them to interpret what was going on. I was required to devise psychometric techniques for making measurable assessments of the effectiveness or otherwise of the Communists' indoctrination programmes on all British prisoners in each of the prison camps. And in order to assess Communist interrogation techniques I was myself trained in the organization of interrogation agencies by Cyril Young (always known as 'John' by his colleagues) and in overt and covert interrogation techniques by the most senior interrogator of M.I.19, the masterly multilingual Major Cyril Hay.

Because of the rapid turnover of service officers I soon found myself to be the longest serving member of the department and I was the only member of the staff who served in A.I.9 for the greater part of its short existence. Because of the rapidity with which A.I.9 was wound up after the cessation of hostilities in Korea, my original official report on the treatment of British p.o.w. was done in a hurry in 1955. After A.I.9 was disbanded and I had returned to Science 4, I found myself approached repeatedly for information by the Cabinet Office, the Foreign Office, various branches of the War Office, a number of Intelligence agencies and even the Ministry of Pensions. I soon realized that the original study was inadequate and consequently in 1956 I was forced into making a far more detailed study in order to answer Ministerial questions, especially about the fates of particular individuals, which of them had been killed under suspicious circumstances and which of them had been tortured to death.

The 1956 version was based upon a wide range of classified and unclassified sources and was completed for military and security purposes. It was an expansion of the 1955 report which had been based upon readily available information and classified and unclassified official sources including the interrogation reports on every one of the British p.o.w. repatriated from Korea. I, personally, carried out long interviews with a number of important people immediately after their repatriation. They included Sir Vivian Holt, the former British Minister to Seoul, Lieut. Colonel J.P. Carne, VC, the former commanding officer of the Gloucestershire Regiment and other officers and servicemen. I also interrogated many of the leading 'progressives' from Camps 1 and 5 shortly after their repatriation. In these interrogations I was given much help by a number of officers of the Intelligence Corps, principally John Young of A.I.9, Cyril Hay of M.I.19,and Alistair West-Watson who had been the head of I.S.9 (K). This version also carried the names of a large number of former p.o.w. who had resisted or co-operated with their captors and included details of various techniques I had devised for assessing the effectiveness of Communist indoctrination and for making security assessments upon individuals. The techniques used to make the assessments must, unfortunately, remain secret, but I have named many of the 'reactionaries' who took part in escape attempts and other acts of defiance.

A very large number of North Korean and Chinese troops of all ranks and arms were captured by the United Nations forces. The interrogation of them by a variety of American intelligence agencies produced a wealth of material on the enemy organizations handling U.N. prisoners of war and upon the state of affairs north of the 38th Parallel.

An unusual and valuable source of information were the notebooks on their political tuition which some British p.o.w. were compelled to keep while in captivity. Some of these came my way as did a few verbatim transcripts of speeches delivered by some of the more prominent members of the Chinese Prisoner of War Corps. Other documentary sources included translations of a vast quantity of captured enemy documents. Other obvious sources were the bulletins issued by the New China News

Agency, propaganda books and pamphlets issued by the ton by the Peking government and reports in the London *Daily Worker*, the British Communist Party newspaper, which, no doubt inadvertently, proved to be surprisingly helpful in providing information. The B.B.C. monitoring service at Caversham regularly supplied transcripts of broadcasts by British p.o.w. over Peking and Pyongyang radio stations.

I re-wrote the 1956 version in the 1960s after I had left the Civil Service and had more time to make a broader study and search of the literature. It benefited from a number of post-war studies by American military psychologists and sociologists and from the transcripts of the trials of a number of Americans, including some of the airmen who had confessed to waging germ warfare.

This present 1999 version has been reorganized and updated in the light of recent history. The variety of the original source materials has, I hope, enabled me to give a balanced account of the mistreatment of the British p.o.w. Also, the passage of almost half a century since the end of the Korean War has led me to make what I hope is a more mature reappraisal of many events.

I must acknowledge the considerable help given to me in compiling the 1955 A.I.9 report by a former p.o.w. in Korea, Captain John De Quidt.

GLOSSARY OF P.O.W. CAMPS NAMES AND NUMBERS

Very considerable difficulty was experienced during the Korean War in locating all the p.o.w. camps set up by three Communist powers and identifying their purposes. For their own nefarious reasons, all three powers refused to indicate the precise whereabouts of many of the camps, especially their penal camps and interrogation centres. Because the camps were often villages or adjacent to villages or parts of villages or requisitioned outbuildings, prisons and schools between villages it was often impossible to name their exact locations. Consequently the peripheral facilities in particular were known by different names to the prisoners incarcerated in the same area, and in the earlier days the numbers given to the camps were sometimes changed.

Throughout this book I have used the names and numbers by which they were known to me during my service with A.I.9. They are as follows:–

TRANSIT CAMPS

NAME	LOCATION
Bean Camp	Suan
Gold Mine or Mining Camp	Soktal-li
The Caves	Kangdong
Halfway House	Munhari
Unknown name	Anju

NORTH KOREAN/RUSSIAN CAMPS

NUMBER	LOCATION	FUNCTION
Camp 9	Kangdong	Notorious camp for all nationalities in the earlier years of the war.

Camp 12	Pyongyang Peace Fighter's School	Indoctrination Centre for selected British and American p.o.w.
Pak's Palace	Pyongyang	NK Army Interrogation Centre in a brickyard.
North Korean & Russian Secret Police prisons.	Pyongyang and Sinuiju	Interrogation Centres for aircrew and escapers.

CHINESE CAMPS

NUMBER	LOCATION	FUNCTION
Camp 1	Chongsong	Main camp for p.o.w. captured at Imjin River.
Camp 2 (1)	Pin Chon-Ni	From Oct '51 main camp for officers and WOs.
Camp 2 (2)	Song-Ni	Penal camp for ORs.
Camp 2 (3)	Chang-Ni	Penal camp for officers and aircrew and a Detailed Interrogation Centre.
Camp 3 (1)	Changsong	Penal camp for ORs undergoing special investigation.
Camp 3 (2)	Songsa-dong	P.O.W. captured after April '51.
Camp 4	Kuuptong	From Aug '51 main camp for sergeants.
Camp 5	Pyoktong	Originally for all ranks captured in January '51 From Oct '51 ORs only. Also HQ of Chinese POW Corps.
Camp 10	Kanggye	Temporary indoctrination school for first p.o.w. captured by Chinese.

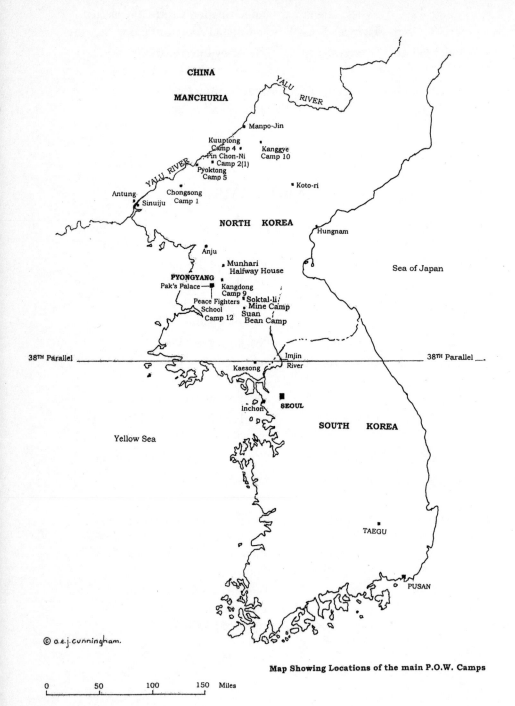

CHINA

MANCHURIA

YALU RIVER

• Manpo-Jin

Kuuptong
Camp 4 •
Pin Chon-Ni
• Camp 2(1)
Pyoktong
Camp 5

Kanggye
Camp 10

• Koto-ri

YALU RIVER

Antung
Sinuiju

Chongsong
Camp 1

NORTH   KOREA

• Hungnam

• Anju

• Munhari
Halfway House

Sea of Japan

PYONGYANG
Pak's Palace

Kangdong
Camp 9
Soktal-li
Mine Camp
Suan
Bean Camp

Peace Fighters
School
Camp 12

38TH Parallel

Imjin
River

38TH Parallel

Kaesong

Inchon

SEOUL

SOUTH   KOREA

Yellow Sea

TAEGU

© a.e.j.cunningham.

PUSAN

Map Showing Locations of the main P.O.W. Camps

0   50   100   150   Miles

1

INTRODUCTION

The Korean War broke out on Sunday 25 June 1950 when the Russian-trained North Korean Army, the so-called North Korean Peoples' Army, crossed the 38th Parallel in great strength and made a rapid advance to the south. Actually there had been some heavy fighting between North and South and much bloodshed for about a year beforehand and both sides had indulged in open political, economic and guerrilla warfare, spying and sabotage against each other.

Since the surrender of Japan on 15 August 1945, at the end of the Second World War, Korea had been split in two at the 38th Parallel. The Soviet Union occupied the north and the Americans the south. Although the Allies had agreed at Potsdam, and reaffirmed at Cairo that at the conclusion of the war Korea would be made a free and independent nation, Soviet Russia, while associating itself with this declaration, had pursued a policy of deliberate obstruction. Prolonged and repeated efforts on the part of the United Nations, to whom the Allies had entrusted the Korean problem, failed to bring about the integration of North and South and free elections. The United Nations therefore ordered a temporary commission of seven nations "to proceed with the observance of elections in all Korea and, if that is impossible, in as much of it as is accessible".

The result was the creation of the Korean Republic under President Syngman Rhee in the South and in the North the Soviet Union set up its own form of government under President Kim Il Sung and claimed that he represented the wishes of all the people of Korea. In fact two-thirds of the population lived in the South. Kim Il Sung was one of nineteen Koreans who had spent the whole of the Second World War in the Soviet Union being groomed for the take-over of Korea.

The withdrawal of Soviet Russian troops from the North and the Americans from the South left the new, bitterly opposed governments growling at each other across the 38th Parallel and it was not long before each began tampering with the affairs of the other. Throughout 1949, when there were only five hundred American troops in the South attached as military advisers to the newly formed Republic of Korea (ROK) army, North Korean guerrillas made repeated incursions across the border, killing a thousand ROK troops and police and wounding two thousand others. On 4 August 1949 the North Korean army invaded the Ongjin peninsula, a sizeable piece of territory on the west coast, south of the 38th Parallel. The attack was repelled, but was launched again without success on 14 October.

In the spring of 1950 a force of six hundred North Koreans made a fighting expedition into the South and were engaged by ROK troops and police at Yongdak. United Nations observers were present and witnessed the annihilation of the invading force. This action was the prelude to the outbreak of general hostilities. It was a feint which successfully drew the ROK forces away from the border area.

The news of the general invasion of the South reached the United Nations Assembly on 25 June, the day of the attack. Member nations were asked "to furnish such assistance to the Republic as was necessary to repel armed attack and restore order". North Korea was called upon to cease hostilities immediately and withdraw. No answer was received to this appeal and on 27 June President Truman ordered the American forces to give ROK forces 'cover and support'. Simultaneously the State Department asked the Soviet Union to use its influence to bring about a withdrawal of the invading forces. This request was ignored.

The next day the British Prime Minister, Clement Attlee, announced that British naval forces would be placed at the disposal of the United States for operations on behalf of the United Nations Security Council. He did not order the army into action until 20 August, by which time the situation in Korea had become critical. Seoul, the South Korean capital, had by then fallen to the invaders who captured a considerable number of European civilians and the staff of the British and many other Western Embassies. These were the first British p.o.w. to fall into enemy hands. That same day President Truman ordered the U.S. army into action. By 7 July the first American troops were in action against the invaders at Suwon. Further substantial reinforcements from America did not reach Korea until two or three weeks later, by which time the North Koreans were ninety miles south of Seoul, Taejon had fallen and Chinju, only ten miles from the south coast, was being threatened. American reinforcements arrived after the fall of Chinju on 31 July. The hard-pressed American and ROK armies were pinned into a small pocket of territory around the southern port of Pusan and were in danger of being driven into the sea.

The first British fighting units, the first battalions of the Middlesex Regiment and the Argyll and Sutherland Highlanders, forming the 27th Brigade, landed in Korea on 29 August, just in time for the heaviest and final North Korean offensive. Other British and Commonwealth troops were soon to follow. Australia and South Africa each contributed a fighter squadron and both Australia and New Zealand eventually sent infantry units.

Early in September the 41st Independent Commando of Royal Marines left the United Kingdom for Korea. Several other nations made, or promised, contributions. Turkey was the first nation to offer troops to the United Nations for service in Korea; Holland provided two thousand infantrymen and France and Belgium each offered a battalion of infantry.

On 15 September 1950 General Douglas MacArthur, the C in C of the United Nations Forces, launched a spectacular offensive. A strong force broke out of the Pusan pocket and attacked the North Koreans at Taegu. Simultaneously an amphibious force, supported by American and British warships, landed at Inchon, the port of Seoul on the west coast, just south of the 38th Parallel. Within a week the two arms of the pincer met, Seoul was recaptured and the bulk of the North Korean army was caught in the trap. A huge number of the enemy was killed and nearly a hundred thousand were taken prisoner by the United Nations Forces. It was a fatal blow to the North Korean regime, which was on the verge of collapse. On 1 October MacArthur called upon the North Koreans to surrender, pointing out that their total defeat was now inevitable.

That same day a Chinese Communist Foreign Ministry spokesman stated that if any United Nations troops crossed the 38th Parallel "the Chinese people would not stand idly by".

Actually, they had not been idle or neutral for several months. Ever since 22 August they had been shooting at United Nations aircraft from the northern shores of the Yalu River, which separates Korea from China. A week after the start of MacArthur's offensive the Chinese shot down an American aircraft. On the following day, 16 October, two thousand Chinese troops, the vanguard of the 42nd Chinese People's Army, described as 'Volunteers', crossed the Yalu River at Wan Po Jin and dashed across mountainous country to the Chosin and Fusan dams where the United States Marines and the 41st Royal Marines Commando were carving up the remnants of the North Korean army in that area.

It seems that the United Nations Command had little inkling of what was already afoot. As late as 24 November, MacArthur launched his much-publicized "Home for Christmas" offensive, the head of which reached the Yalu River, presumably in ignorance of the fact that something like two hundred thousand Chinese troops were already in Korea deploying for a devastating counter-attack. The blow fell early in December when a massive Chinese attack sliced through the centre of the United Nations lines and fanned out on either side to cut off their retreat. The U.N. troops were hastily withdrawn intact from the north-west of Korea, but in the north-east considerable difficulty was encountered in evacuating U.N. and ROK troops through the port of Hungman. The British and American marines in the area of the Chosin reservoir were left out on a limb and their rearguard of about three hundred men, including twenty-five Royal Marines, was ambushed and captured by the Chinese at a place called Koto-ri. Thus did the first group of British troops fall into enemy hands.

By 23 December the battlefront was back on the 38th Parallel and hasty arrangements were being made to defend the South Korean capital. Among the defenders was the Royal Ulster Rifles.

The general retreat continued, hampered by three million refugees. During this precarious period the ROK government launched a violent campaign against alleged traitors and spies, and the British troops witnessed the round-up and mass execution of a large number of Korean men, women and children. Shocked by the incident, the officers of the Royal Ulster Rifles intervened and protested to the United Nations representatives. Representations were made to the South Korean President, Syngman Rhee, who gave them the cynical assurance that in future the victims would be shot individually and not en masse! The incident made a profound impression on the British troops who almost immediately afterwards went into battle to defend this regime.

On 3 January 1951, in bitter weather, the U.N. evacuated Seoul, leaving the Royal Ulster Rifles and supporting units, including tanks, to cover the retreat. Over three hundred of them were killed or captured in this action. More than half of those captured were severely wounded. The Chinese offensive came to a halt shortly afterwards.

In the Spring of 1951 the U.N. forces counter-attacked and re-established the front along the 38th Parallel. Several more British units reached Korea and were deployed thirty miles north of Seoul, along the Imjin River. Several admirable eye-witness accounts have been published of the Imjin River battle, among them that of Captain (subsequently General Sir Anthony) Farrar-Hockley in his book *The Edge of the Sword*.

It is not necessary to give details of it here except to say that the 29th Brigade under Brigadier Brodie had the job of defending sixteen thousand yards of front. Three infantry battalions were involved, the Gloucestershire Regiment, the Royal Northumberland Fusiliers and the Royal Ulster Rifles, supported by the 45th Field Regiment, Royal Artillery and the Centurion tanks of the 8th Royal Irish Hussars. Also under Brodie's command was a Belgian battalion, making a total force of about two thousand personnel.

On 22 April the Chinese launched a series of phased offensives the main weight of which struck the British sector. The Glosters were outflanked and after three days of bitter fighting ran out of ammunition. Attempts to relieve them and to supply them from the air failed. On 25 April their commanding officer, Lieut. Colonel J.P. Carne, received permission to abandon his positions and gave orders to his men to make their own ways back to U.N. lines which were now sixteen miles to the rear. Out of a total strength of about eight hundred only forty of the Glosters managed to regain friendly lines. The rest were either killed or captured.

The Royal Northumberland Fusiliers and the Royal Ulster Rifles fought with equal determination against overwhelming odds and sustained heavy casualties. But, unlike the Glosters, attempts to relieve them succeeded and the majority were extricated from their beleaguered positions, although their rearguard was cut off and about two hundred of them were killed or captured.

This third and largest group of British personnel to fall into enemy hands included officers and men of five regiments, three infantry, one tank, one artillery and their supporting services, about eight hundred altogether. Many of them died of their wounds within the next three days.

The Imjin River battle was one of the last great battles of the Korean War. Shortly afterwards the line settled down to trench warfare along the 38th Parallel and remained there until the armistice was signed on 27 July 1953. The 29th Brigade was relieved and other famous British regiments replaced those that had fought during the crucial campaigns. Between the summer of 1951 and the summer of 1953 there was desultory fighting culminating in a sudden flare-up in the last two weeks of the war as both sides endeavoured to gain vital scraps of territory. In these two years less than two hundred British and Commonwealth troops fell into enemy hands compared with more than a thousand in the preceding year.

Throughout the war the United Nations had consistently sought a cease-fire and for a year there was no response from the Communists. It was not until 23 May, when the Chinese had regained the territory lost by the North Koreans, that the Soviet Union intimated that a cease-fire might be possible. At an interview with the American ambassador in Moscow, the Soviet Deputy Foreign Minister, Mr Andrei Gromyko, intimated that a strictly military arrangement between commanders on the spot in Korea would be acceptable. He left no doubt that the Communists would not entertain any agreement involving political or territorial issues. Subsequently negotiations were initiated by the United Nations C in C, General Ridgway, who had replaced MacArthur, and, after two and a half years of wrangling point by point, resulted in the repatriation of sick and wounded p.o.w. in April 1953, an armistice on 7 July and a general exchange of p.o.w. in September of the same year.

One of the last cruel acts of the Chinese was to release in the exchange of supposedly sick and wounded British p.o.w. a high proportion who had no serious wounds or sickness. Classified as having anxiety neuroses, they were in fact the hard-core collaborators who were released early in order to tell the world how well their captors had treated all prisoners.

From these hoaxsters and the genuine sick and wounded it was learned that there were very many more men still in the camps whose genuinely serious illnesses and wounds qualified them for early repatriation according to the agreement that had been made with the Communists. These unfortunate men had to await the main exchange of prisoners six months later when once again the same propaganda trick was perpetrated. The bulk of those first released were collaborators who could be relied upon to feed the Western press with glowing stories of life in captivity and to praise their captors for their supposed 'leniency'.

Even then the Communists had not played their last trick. Although no United Kingdom personnel were concerned, a number of Americans and one officer of the Royal Canadian Air Force were retained as hostages in Mukden, Manchuria. The R.C.A.F. officer was not repatriated for more than a year after the armistice was signed and some of the American Air Force aviators and technicians were kidnapped by the Russians and disappeared for ever into the Gulag Archipelago.

It is impossible to determine the exact number of British personnel who fell into enemy hands. There are several reasons for this. In the confusion of battle men are apt to disappear or are unrecognizable from their mangled remains. Groups get separated from their units at critical moments and it is not always possible to trace their whereabouts or fates, especially if, during the immediate aftermath of a battle, the enemy shoots a few prisoners for failing to give them information. In Korea the best estimates were that 1,148 British servicemen were captured alive, a figure which does not include those who when last seen lay mortally wounded on the battlefields. Nine hundred and seventy-eight were repatriated, comprising forty Army officers, two Naval officers and one RAF officer, 915 O.Rs, eighteen Royal Marines and two naval ratings. The balance of eleven officers and 159 O.Rs, that is about 15%, perished in captivity. This compares with 6,656 American army personnel captured alive, of whom 3,323, i.e. approximately 50%, perished in captivity.

2

STALINISM vs MAOISM

RUSSIAN, NORTH KOREAN AND CHINESE P.O.W. POLICIES

Never before had British troops fallen into the hands of a Communist enemy and the treatment they received in Korea caught them completely unprepared.

When hostilities commenced there was much speculation in Whitehall about how the North Koreans would treat their prisoners. At first opinions were equally divided between two theories. There were those who considered that they would be as barbarous as they had been as part of the Japanese army in the Second World War, in which their prisoners had been starved, beaten and put to work as slaves, a theory which gained credence as news of atrocities began to filter through to London. The other theory was that, as a Soviet Russian satellite state, they would pursue a Russian policy, and we had plenty of evidence of that from the ongoing interrogations of German p.o.w. currently still being repatriated from Russia. Their treatment was only marginally less brutal than the Japanese. The Russians had ruthlessly exploited them for their intelligence value before using them as slaves. However, nobody as yet knew the full extent of Soviet influence above the 38th Parallel and few knew that the reservations which the Soviet Union had made when signing the Geneva Convention were deliberate devices for escaping from its terms when it suited them.

The intervention of the Chinese produced further complications. Communist China was not a signatory to the Geneva Convention and nobody seemed to know how they treated prisoners of war. They had only recently completed the conquest of mainland China and received diplomatic recognition. And nobody could have foreseen that they would take over the custody of the majority of p.o.w. north of the 38th Parallel and that their policy would eventually predominate and edge the Russians and North Koreans into a minority role.

It took weeks of research to find useful evidence of the p.o.w. policies of the main belligerents and the outcome was surprising.

The Russian policy differed materially from the Chinese, as did the organizations which put them into effect. The Soviet policy, if such it could be called, originated from a decree issued by Stalin in May 1942. It ordered the secret police, the MVD (forerunner of the KGB), to assume responsibility for p.o.w. interrogation and exploitation, a task previously done by the Red Army. The latter, well aware that Stalin regarded p.o.w. as deserters deserving to be shot for failing to fight to the death, and goaded by Nazi atrocities, was bent upon revenge. German p.o.w. were slaughtered and abused in such numbers that Moscow was deprived of a valuable source of intelligence and forced labour, badly needed to replace their own nationals transferred to the Red Army from the slave labour camps. The Gulag slave labour system was pivotal to the entire Russian economy, especially for the extraction of raw materials from the mines, quarries and forests. From May 1942 the MVD rectified the army's mistakes with ruthless efficiency. It assumed control of tactical and strategic interrogations and swallowed all p.o.w. camps into the slave labour system. Several million Germans were compelled to make a handsome contribution to the Soviet war effort and the information ruthlessly wrung from German technical and scientific personnel was largely responsible for the rapid advances made in these fields by the Russians during the Second World War. When the end of the war was in sight the Russians sought ways of retaining these valuable reserves. They exploited a loophole in the Four Power Agreement they had signed in Potsdam which allowed all parties to retain war criminals until they had completed their sentences for their crimes. Throughout 1945 and for years thereafter the weight of the MVD interrogation effort was devoted into converting as many German p.o.w. as possible into 'war criminals' so that they could be held almost indefinitely as slave labour in the Gulag Archipelago. By this device Russia was also able to hang on to a large number of Japanese p.o.w., including Koreans who had served in the Imperial Army.

The retention of prisoners on the pretext of war crimes must be emphasized because throughout the Korean War the Communists accused all the U.N. prisoners of being war criminals, compounding Western fears that they might be retained as slaves after the cessation of hostilities.

As the Second World War was drawing to a close, the Russians introduced compulsory political education for all nationalities of Axis p.o.w.; they had to attend classes after a heavy day's work, and those who progressed were sent to Anti-Fascist (Antifa) schools to train them further

9

in the Communist philosophy. It was from this scheme that the Russians selected prisoners for grooming for office in the organs of state after their seizure of power in the East European states.

When the Japanese surrendered in August 1945 the Russians produced nineteen Korean Communists who re-entered Korea as part of the occupation forces. They had lived for years in Russia and become Soviet citizens. Headed by Kim Il Sung, they formed the core of a puppet government backed up by Korean former p.o.w. from the Antifa schools. The Russians sat at their elbows even after North Korea declared itself an independent republic on 9 September 1948 and were there as advisors throughout the Korean War, though none were captured by the United Nations forces.

The new Korean People's Republic was modelled strictly on the Soviet pattern where power was equally split between the Party, the Army and the Secret Police. Each of these departments, headed by Soviet-Koreans, possessed departments that were concerned with the handling of United Nations p.o.w. Their activities were co-ordinated by a joint Russian-Korean organization known as the P.O.W. Administration, through which the Russians influenced the treatment of prisoners. The Administration had its headquarters in Pyongyang, the North Korean capital, and its Director was a Russian officer of the Far Eastern MVD, a man who called himself Colonel Andrep. There were two vice-chiefs, one a Russian MVD officer, Lieut. Colonel Bakusope, the other a Soviet Korean, Kim Il, allegedly the brother of the North Korean President Kim Il Sung. The head of the Secretariat was another Russian MVD officer named Takayarankayasky, otherwise known as 'One-Eye'. The Administration was responsible for the interrogation, education and exploitation of prisoners of war according to the Russian policy through its executive agencies.

The agencies with which British p.o.w. most frequently came into contact were the main military intelligence department and the military commissars of the Bureau of Politics. Some prisoners, principally aircrew, escapers and diplomatic personnel, fell into the hands of the security police, the North Korean equivalent of the Russian MVD.

The Army's detailed interrogation centre consisted of a complex of caves, tunnels, holes and corners centring on a brickyard in the suburbs of Pyongyang and was known to the p.o.w. as Pak's Palace, after the name of the brutal Korean interrogator, Major Pak. Although this centre was ostensibly commanded by a North Korean Colonel by the name of Lee, and later by Major Pak, there is evidence that it was directed by several

Russians who occasionally interrogated some of the British p.o.w.

The Political Bureau was responsible for the indoctrination of prisoners and propaganda warfare and ran an indoctrination school in the south-eastern suburbs of the capital. It was known to the prisoners as the Peace Fighters' Camp, officially known as Camp No. 12. This centre was run on the lines of the Russian Antifa schools, though it had a much more limited objective. It was here that a small but very vociferous group of British and American p.o.w. were trained to act as a political front orga-nization called "The U.S.- British War Prisoners Peace Organization", allegedly speaking for all the U.N. prisoners, including those in the Chinese-controlled camps, issuing appeals and petitions condemning the war in the world's press and making broadcasts over Pyongyang radio. No Russians were seen at this centre which was run by a North Korean, Colonel Kim, under the direct supervision of General Kim Il of the P.O.W. Administration.

The detailed interrogation centre of the North Korean security police was located in a modern concrete building in the centre of Pyongyang, near the central prison. Many of its prisoners had been routed through a series of secret police prisons to Sinuiji which lies in the extreme north-west of Korea right on the border with Manchuria with easy access to the Manchurian port of Antung. After being screened at Sinuiji some were transferred to the central prison in Pyongyang which was equipped with a torture chamber. Diplomatic prisoners, including George Blake, were put into a special camp for 'important (civilian) prisoners' in another border town, Man po, and later shifted to a nearby farmhouse where they were interrogated by Russians, North Koreans and Chinese.

The division of responsibility between three agencies within the North Korean P.O.W. Administration led to body-snatching from each other and confusion and rivalry which led to a number of instances of Russian advisors rebuking high ranking North Koreans.

The Chinese p.o.w. policy differed greatly in principle and practice from that of the Russian/North Korean. But at the outbreak of the Korean War there was a tendency in official circles to regard China as just one more Russian satellite state. However, anybody who has read a little of Chinese history will know that this was far from being the case. There were early theoretical differences between Russian and Chinese versions of Communism. Lenin's version was based upon the urban proletariat, but at that time China had a predominantly peasant population. For centuries the unfortunate peasants had been victimized by feudal war lords and various political factions which had made central government

11

almost impossible. Amidst this chaos Mao Tse-tung's Agrarian Reform Movement achieved spectacular success among the destitute peasants and in February 1930 after initial experiments in Hunan, Mao founded the Kiangsi Provincial Soviet Government in a large area on the Kiangsi-Hunan border. It was a small Communist state in the interior of China in an area remote from the authority of the Kuomintang regime of Chiang Kai-shek. Almost at once it came under fierce attack by surrounding warlords and the Central Government forces. Mao realized that "Power comes out of the barrel of a gun", and that in an environment in which military power was decisive he needed a strong army to ensure his survival. At first he trained peasants as guerrillas, but he soon realized that he needed a regular army.

Traditionally the Chinese soldier was a peasant-bandit who would follow any cause that promised loot and he was liable to desert at the sound of a cannon. Mao realized that such men were useless unless they could be instilled with a belief in the cause for which they were fighting. He therefore sent his troops to school and indoctrination formed a major part of their training. He then used these troops to raid rural areas around the Kiangsi Soviet, capturing as many enemy prisoners as he could from the armies of the Central Government and the war lords. But instead of abusing these prisoners they were treated leniently, educated and then recruited into his own army. In a short period the strength of his regular Red Army grew to 30,000 by 1931.

Here, then, we have the origins of the Chinese Communists' p.o.w. policy, which clearly predates that of the Soviet Russians. It was a policy of so-called 'Leniency' which was later used with great effect against both Kuomintang and Japanese troops during the Second World War. During that war the Communists were supposed to have a neutrality and territorial agreement with Nationalist Chinese forces against the common Japanese enemy. After the war the Nationalists accused the Communists of devoting the greater part of their effort to waging war on them and complained bitterly that they had been attacked by the Communists in Japanese-occupied areas in breach of the neutrality agreement. They also complained that their troops captured by the Communists had been indoctrinated before being pressed into service with the Red Army. The Communists countered by accusing the Nationalists of deserting en masse to the Japanese, who subsequently used them to fight the Communists.

During the course of eight years' warfare against the Japanese (September 1937 – May 1945) the Communists claim to have captured 73,832 Nationalist prisoners, whom they called 'puppets of the Japanese'.

12

In a long report dated 22 June 1944, describing these successes, General Yeh Chien-ying, Chief of Staff of the 18ᵗʰ Communist Army Group, stated:–

> Our policy is not to slaughter captives but to give them preferential treatment as brothers, allowing them to remain or to leave as they prefer; at the same time we are carrying out untiring anti-fascist political education among them, releasing them to go back or retaining those who are willing to remain. All this has a great effect in weakening the fighting morale of the enemy.

This, then, explicitly stated, has been the Chinese Communists p.o.w. policy. It originated in the Kiangsi Soviet in 1927 and was used consistently until the Nationalists were defeated on mainland China in 1949. In 1950 it was used for the first time against Western troops in Korea and a variation of it appeared almost simultaneously in Indo-China where it was called the Policy of Clemency of Ho Chi Minh.

Since the earliest days of the Kiangsi Soviet Mao Tse-tung relied upon his army to spread the gospel and consolidate his power. By tradition the Army is omnipotent and there is no division of power as there was under the Soviet Russian system. It is the army that is responsible for security and for the ideological education of its own troops as well as the civilian population and prisoners of war.

The entry of the Chinese into the Korean War on 20 October 1950 must have been viewed with some misgivings by the North Koreans and their Russian allies. Since the end of the Second World War Russia had expended considerable treasure and effort upon building a regime of its own brand of Communism in North Korea and had declared it a People's Republic a year before the Chinese Communists had completed the conquest of their own country. From the moment the vanguard of the Chinese 42ⁿᵈ Army, describing itself as the Chinese People's Volunteers, crossed the dams of the Yalu River, the authority of the Russians and their brand of Communism was threatened, as was their role as the traditional leaders of world Communism. The ability of Mao to field a huge army so soon after the conquest of its own country must have shaken the Russians as much as it did the Western powers. With only a seventeen-mile frontier between Russia and Korea in the far north-east of the country, an area through which the Chinese were now pouring troops into Korea, the Russian advisers must have cast very uneasy glances towards their own back door. Within a few months there was not an inch of territory north

13

of the 38th Parallel that was not swarming with Chinese troops and their military supremacy over the Russians and North Koreans was no longer in any doubt. Not a grain of rice or a bullet could be moved from Russia into Korea without passing through Chinese-occupied territory and the North Koreans were no longer even caretakers in their own country. It was ironic that the Chinese were dependent upon the Russians for much of their military hardware and were outraged that the Russians were making them pay for every bit of it. As the Chinese were taking the brunt of the fighting they were also taking most of the prisoners of war.

From the very beginning the Chinese came to some sort of agreement with their allies over the sharing and handling of p.o.w. The vice-chief of the political department of the Chinese People's Volunteers, a man named Tu Pyong, was attached to the Russian/North Korean P.O.W. Administration in Pyongyang and must have been greatly disconcerted by the fundamental differences in their respective p.o.w. policies. The North Koreans' brutal treatment of the prisoners was a flat contradiction of the traditional Chinese Lenient Policy.

In Korea the only Chinese organization dealing with p.o.w. was an army formation called the Prisoner of War Corps and its function was the same as it had been in the days of the Kiangsi Soviet. The Prisoner of War Corps of the Chinese People's Volunteers was commanded by General Wang Yang Kung who established his headquarters in Camp No.5 at Pyoktong, on the Yalu River. The Corps had two components. The first ran the p.o.w. camps and the second comprised p.o.w. Guard Companies whose duties were escorting prisoners to the permanent camps and subsequently guarding them. The senior officers of the Corps were no more volunteers than a fatigue squad in a British Army cookhouse. They were veterans of numerous campaigns, hardened Communists without a grain of humour in their characters. Few of them could speak English and those who could preferred to conceal the fact and addressed the prisoners through interpreters. Many of the interpreters were also old campaigners who had acquired their knowledge of the English language and customs at American, English, Malayan and Hong Kong universities and mission schools.

When the Chinese intervened in Korea they were, on their own admission, desperately short of interpreters with sufficient military experience and knowledge of the American way of life. As the p.o.w. population rapidly increased through American defeats these difficulties were accentuated and were finally overcome by conscripting language students from their own universities. As one of these young conscripts told his prisoners, he had been studying English when the war broke out and his professor had "patriotically volunteered the entire faculty" for service in Korea. He was therefore a genuine volunteer!

In Korea the Prisoner of War Corps was initially severely handicapped by the lack of the elementary facilities due to the devastation and to their strained relations with their North Korean and Russian allies, both of whom were in a position to make things awkward for the Chinese invaders since they controlled such facilities as had survived in the way of accommodation, transport and communications. Nevertheless, the Chinese were old campaigners and were very experienced in making the best of existing resources.

The Prisoner of War Corps possessed no conventional detailed interrogation centres comparable to those set up by both sides in the Second World War. They used whatever accommodation was available in the transit camps and prison camps or villages near the camps, and where specialist knowledge was needed to question special prisoner categories and evaluate the information they seem to have used teams of peripatetic specialists travelling from camp to camp. The exceptions were the camps where American aircrews were assembled for questioning on their alleged use of germ warfare and where they were forced into making damning confessions. But even here there were no special facilities, no static installations comparable to those used in Europe.

One had to search very hard indeed to find evidence of Russian interference with the activities of the Chinese. There were one or two isolated instances of attempts by the Russians to give the Chinese advice and on these occasions the Chinese showed their irritation in no uncertain fashion.

As will be seen from the following chapters the essential difference between the Chinese and North Korean treatment of prisoners was the amount of effort which the Chinese expended upon the utterly ruthless and brutal exploitation of the U.N. prisoners, not, as might have been expected, for military and other kinds of intelligence or for slave labour, as the Russians and Japanese had done in World War II, but for purely *political* and world-wide *propaganda* objectives and for tactical advantages in their negotiation of peace terms. Moreover, unlike the North Koreans, who simply caged their prisoners and left them to their own devices after interrogating them or using them for labour, the Chinese went out of their way to force all their prisoners to organize their daily lives on Communist lines and live under a Communist social system. The entire Chinese treatment of the British p.o.w. was geared to these ends,

15

which had never before been encountered by our armed services. Consequently it caught them completely unprepared and devoid of any organized counter-measures, especially in respect of the close personal attention to the political inclinations of every individual prisoner.

The incompatibility of the two very different p.o.w. policies became abundantly obvious to the very considerable number of prisoners who were passed from Chinese to North Korean custody. The Chinese promises of lenient treatment seemed a cruel joke to those taken over by or transferred to the custody of the North Koreans. Those who survived were ultimately transferred back into Chinese custody where the treatment was indeed lenient by comparison, but only if they were prepared to learn the 'truth'. Otherwise they discovered that the Lenient Policy and the Chinese brand of Communism was as savage and as brutal as it had been in the North Korean jails.

3

DEATH ON THE MARCH

Most of the prisoners who perished in Korea died early in captivity, that is to say in the period between capture and evacuation on foot to the permanent p.o.w. camps near the Yalu River, two hundred and sixty miles to the north, to the border with China. Both the North Korean and the Chinese Communist armies regarded capture as a disgrace and made it a struggle for survival which taught the survivors that their captors were callously indifferent to their fates. On average during the evacuation period fourteen per cent of the British p.o.w. and forty per cent of the Americans died as a result of exposure, unattended wounds and diseases contracted in filthy, overcrowded accommodation in the hovels, caves, holes and corners that served as transit camps. It was a phase of captivity that none of the survivors will ever forget and it did much to determine their early behaviour in the permanent p.o.w. camps.

During the Second World War, in the Korean War and in the war with the French in Indo-China a shocking percentage of prisoners captured by the Communists died in transit to prison camps. The Communists excused these casualties by blaming them on adverse and unfortunate local circumstances and to supply difficulties due to enemy bombing, and they insisted that the diseases suffered by the p.o.w. had been contracted prior to capture.

In almost every war the evacuation period is one of extreme danger and hardship for prisoners. In Korea it was exacerbated by the climate and the devastation of the countryside. But, even allowing for these factors, much of the prisoners' suffering was the direct result of malevolence and deliberate neglect and suggests that it was a deliberate Communist policy intended to reduce their number, destroy prisoners' morale, make them compliant and emphasize their dependency upon the 'leniency' of their captors.

Prior to the Chinese intervention and for a while afterwards the North Koreans were responsible for the care of all prisoners. In their first advance into the South they captured several hundred young American soldiers, dressed in their summer uniforms. They also captured a considerable number of civilians including Western diplomatic personnel. Thus the first British prisoners to be captured by the North Koreans were the staff of the British Legation including the British Minister to the South Korean government, Captain Vivian Holt, his Consul, Norman Owen, his Vice-Consul, George Blake, who was actually a Secret Service man, eventually to be 'turned' into a spy for the Soviet Union while a p.o.w., and many civilians. These included Commissioner Lord of the Salvation Army, a fluent Korean speaker, and Bishop Cooper, Father Hunt and other missionaries. The British Minister and several members of his staff were taken by car into Pyongyang, to the headquarters of the North Korean Security Police where they were questioned in the presence of a Russian MVD officer. Afterwards they were put into a camp for important prisoners, a school surrounded by barbed wire, where they were later joined by senior members of the staff of the French, Swiss and other European Legations, and even an East German communist. This party, which included a badly wounded British correspondent of *The Observer*, Philip Deane, and many elderly missionaries and nuns, had been kept in filthy conditions in a so-called camp in Seoul, but the city had been bombed and was considered unsafe. So they were all moved north to Pyongyang to join the other diplomats. But the capital was also under American air attacks so on 5 September the prisoners were put on a train which took five days and nights to reach its destination, Man po, a frontier town on the Yalu River and a crossing point into China. This camp was an old Japanese quarantine barracks and was already housing bedraggled American army p.o.w.

Four months after the fall of Seoul the United Nations forces broke out of the Pusan pocket and landed at Inchon, forcing the North Koreans to make a lightning retreat. The U.N. forces almost reached the Yalu River; the prisoners in Man po could hear their guns and see their aircraft overhead and had hopes of being liberated. However, instead of being left by the retreating North Korean army, they were moved to a safer area. In bitter weather the party of diplomats, elderly priests and nuns and hundreds of bedraggled American troops still wearing the rags of their summer uniforms, minus their boots which had been stolen by their guards, were forced to march for fifteen miles through the snow and the mountains. This column was under the command of a ruthless North Korean officer known by his victims as 'The Tiger'. Any elderly or sick prisoner who failed to keep up with the rapid pace of the column was taken into a ditch and shot in the back of the head by The Tiger who also executed many of the American p.o.w. "to reduce their number".

After his repatriation, Sir Vivian Holt gave his unique opinion of this period. In his view, The Tiger had a very difficult job evacuating a column that contained many important and aged prisoners through a country on the verge of collapse. He had to find whatever he could in the way of food and accommodation in the devastated countryside. With the American army hard on his heels, he could not afford to have any stragglers. If he had left them by the wayside, Sir Vivian said, they would have died anyway, either from the cold or from their illnesses and infirmities, or would have been killed by the bombarding American aircraft or ground forces. So they were shot in the back of the head and left by the wayside. The conditions of the survivors deteriorated with every mile of this march, the most publicized of all the so-called 'Death Marches'. They were kept in temporary accommodation for only a few days before being marched back to Man po. On the way they saw large numbers of Chinese troops pouring into the country. Man po was still burning from American air attacks so the party was moved again in temperatures falling to 70 degrees below zero to a filthy p.o.w. camp at Hadjang. More than a hundred of the American p.o.w. died on this leg of the march. Hadjang was a death camp already housing American p.o.w. Vivian Holt and Norman Owen nearly died of diseases and many of the civilians did die after being dragged, protesting, to what was known to the prisoners as the 'death houses', which their captors described as a hospital.

In the squalor of Hadjang the North Koreans had the effrontery to subject their diplomatic prisoners to a programme of compulsory indoc-trination, but were outwitted by their prisoners who were very well versed in classical Communist works and could quote them from memory to refute their indoctrinators' arguments. The death rate reached such appalling levels that the North Koreans finally realized the risks to their diplomatic prisoners and moved the most important of them to a heated farmhouse near Man po. It was here, in the autumn of 1951, that specialist Russian and Chinese interrogators arrived, including a Russian MVD officer, Gregory Kuzmitch, who 'turned' George Blake into a spy for the Russians. (Kuzmitch defected to the Americans shortly after the end of the Korean War!)

Following the entry of the Chinese into the war the United Nations forces were driven back to the 38th Parallel and by Christmas preparations were again being made for the defence of Seoul. By this time the North Koreans already controlled a chain of makeshift transit camps situated at intervals along the main trunk route from the 38th Parallel northwards to the Yalu River where they also had a few static p.o.w. camps or accommodation that could be used as camps. These camps, moreover, were under the protection of an umbrella of Russian Mig fighters.

The Chinese Guard Companies, whose map-reading abilities were dreadful, soon discovered that supplies and accommodation during moves between transit camps depended entirely upon the goodwill or malevolence of the local North Korean authorities. The uneasy relations between the two Communist authorities was at the expense of the p.o.w., with the result that the prisoners were starved almost to death and were compelled to march unnecessary distances when their Chinese guards lost their sense of direction. If any of the prisoners fell by the wayside they were left to the mercy of the North Korean army and the civilian population (not all of whom were vindictive). The net effect was that most of the p.o.w. who fell by the wayside were sick and wounded, escapers and small parties which had become separated from their Chinese guards. All these prisoners gravitated, eventually, towards camps in the vicinity of Pyongyang, the North Korean capital.

The route taken by all the main evacuation columns was essentially the same and all were compelled to march across rugged and mountainous terrain. For much of the distance the route ran parallel to the main south-to-north communications system that runs up the western side of the country. All along the route there were villages that served as staging posts, but there were five that served as primitive transit camps where the p.o.w. were allowed to rest for periods varying between two or three days to several weeks. These, in the order in which they were approached were Suan, known as the Bean Camp, Soktal-li, known as the Gold Mine or Mining Camp, Kangdong, known as The Caves, Munhari, known as Halfway House, and Anju. At the latter the columns had to cross a bridge spanning a sizeable river, the Chongch'on, north of which the country was mountainous and relatively sparsely populated. For unknown reasons not a single British p.o.w. could give a description of the route from Anju to their permanent camps.

The time taken to complete the journey varied from column to column. In January the men who had been captured after the battle for Seoul suffered exceptionally not only because of the severe weather but also from deficiencies in the Chinese organization of their evacuation. None of the prisoners from this column has published his experiences in captivity but one, believed to be Corporal W. Massey of the Royal Ulster Rifles, kept a diary of this period and smuggled it out of captivity, upon repatriation. Written in ink in minute writing on both sides of a single piece of thin rice paper, it records the names of many of those captured alive with him, eighty-three men and five officers, Major M.D. Ryan, Captain James Majury and Lieutenant Bruford-Davies of the Royal Ulster Rifles, the M.O. Captain A.M. Ferrie and Captain A.H.C.Gibbon of the Royal Artillery. It gives an interesting insight into their plight over the next few months. It begins on 3 January 1951 with the entry:-

Had great hopes all afternoon. We were moving south of the Ham River but when we went to move at 10.30 pm we were ambushed. We fought it out for four and a half hours. Then we had to surrender. It was a terrible day. I was captured by the Chinese.

Every few days for the next three months he made an entry:–

4th Jan. Spent all day in a little room. No food. Moved when it got dark.
5th. Spent all day in a big shed.
6th Moved to a new room. Marching all night. Snowing very hard.

It is known that it took the Chinese a long time to assemble a column for evacuation and that after the battle the British troops were rounded up in penny numbers and assembled in small groups, many of which were taken over by the North Koreans. The enemy insisted on compelling the prisoners to leave their non-ambulatory wounded on the battlefield and in one instance forcibly prevented them from going to the aid of men lying trapped under burning vehicles. The more seriously wounded were shot by their captors who did not possess the medical facilities necessary to save their lives, but the survivors saw this as pitiless indifference to the sufferings of the helpless and a calculated inducement to many badly injured men to try to keep up with their comrades. Many of the Chinese escorts lost their way and marched their prisoners about the forward areas for days, seeking shelter in local villages at night. Many parties changed hands between the Chinese and North Koreans, some several times. For one group it was two weeks before they and their Chinese escorts reached the assembly area and some of the wounded were sent by train into Pyongyang where there was a Chinese military hospital. Ultimately many of these men fell into North Korean hands and experienced dreadful treatment for weeks, sometimes for months, before they were handed back to the Chinese, if they survived. One party of nine wounded prisoners was marched back to the battlefield where they were compelled to clear it of debris and dig bunkers and defences for the enemy troops. One British prisoner was employed for a month as a dustman in the occupied South Korean capital, Seoul. Another, Rifleman J. Hibbert, spent eighteen months altogether in North Korean hands and for much of this time worked in a slave labour gang. Several other British p.o.w. were last seen ragged, thin and begging for food, among a gang of South Korean slave labourers in the vicinity of Pyongyang. Yet others were employed by the North Koreans between periods of interrogation in the Pyongyang marshalling yards unloading ammunition trains under American air attacks. Another group was taken to Pyongyang airfield and made to locate and defuse unexploded bombs. About thirty of the British troops taken into Pyongyang city disappeared and were never seen again.

Once the prisoners arrived in the assembly area they were joined by some American prisoners for the eight-week march to the north. They marched mostly at night to avoid being attacked from the air and hid up during the day in whatever shelter was available, in villages, railway tunnels, bunkers or simply in ditches in bitter weather. On 3 February, a month after capture, the column reached the first of the so-called transit camps at Suan, situated about forty-five miles south-east of the North Korean capital. It was known to all prisoners as the Bean Camp because their diet comprised a daily handful of beans. It had been a small gold-mining community until attacked and partially destroyed by United Nations aircraft. Now all that were left were derelict native huts with broken walls, into which the prisoners were crammed.

Massey's diary records:–

Just another day waiting for a bowl of rice. Moving tomorrow 150 miles.
Finished 4th night marching. In a big barn freezing all night.
Food getting worse. Still marching.
Finished the march after ten nights marching. In a new camp.

During the next few days he wrote:–

Had my pay book taken from me and also my diary (pocket diary).
Got my pay book and diary back.
Got good food for the first time in weeks; 1 bean cake, 1 bowl of
bean soup.
My stomach very sore. A lot of the boys have dyrio (diarrhoea)
Very bad with stomach today. Going to latrine 30 times a day.

Even the healthy p.o.w. now began to go down with dysentery in
increasing numbers. The repeated requests of the Senior British Officer,
Major M.D. Ryan of the Royal Ulster Rifles, to contact the Red Cross for
medical and other essential supplies were sharply rebuffed. The Red Cross
was branded as an 'Imperialist Spy Organization' that used its special
status to infiltrate agents into foreign territory. Nevertheless, Ryan
persisted and was able to obtain extra accommodation and fuel to heat
it, into which the sick and injured were placed. Despite his efforts, many
of the prisoners, mainly Americans, but including eight British prisoners,
died of dysentery, pneumonia and unattended wounds.

Soon after reaching Suan most, if not all, the prisoners were interviewed
by English-speaking Chinese who enquired into their political affinities.
Many of them were issued with a document that was to become un-
pleasantly familiar to all the prisoners in Korea. It was a primitive
autobiographical inventory containing thirty or forty questions. Several
versions were issued by the Chinese during the war under various titles
such as 'An Outline of your Autobiography'. They were all essentially the
same and required the prisoner to give a detailed description of himself,
a history of his life from birth to the time of capture, listing schools, occupations, military service and the names of all his relatives and their ages,
schooling, occupations, political affinities and religious beliefs.

This faced each prisoner with a dilemma. Every British soldier was
instructed to give only his name, rank and number if captured and no
other information if interrogated by the enemy. But this policy assumes
that all prisoners will know when they are being interrogated and what
sort of information has any military significance. The Chinese autobiographical inventories skated neatly round these points. The prisoners
were very unsure as to whether a questionnaire constitutes an interrogation. Some prisoners took it to be a p.o.w. registration form of the sort
used by the Red Cross to identify the captives and their next of kin. Many
of the p.o.w., on repatriation, claimed that they had not been interrogated
at Suan.

Some of the p.o.w. answered all the questions. Others completed only the personal questions. Some were extremely cautious and refused to answer the questions. Yet others gave flippant answers and reduced the whole matter to the ridiculous. They were later to pay for their flippancy when the Chinese re-issued these forms at regular intervals. Then the humorists and fabricators had to explain, if they could, the discrepancies to hard-nosed and ruthless interrogators. The collective result was that the enemy accumulated enough information to be able to identify the Communist Party members among the prisoners and others with left-wing tendencies, information which, as we shall see, seems to have been shared with the North Koreans.

At least eighteen British prisoners, including eleven from the tank regiment, the 8th Irish Hussars, were subjected to more searching interrogation for information of a military nature. The tank crews were asked for technical information about their Cromwell and Centurion tanks. When they declined to answer they were not mistreated; they were warned of the fate awaiting liars and were shown the answers in copies of the servicing manuals of the tanks! Thereafter few of these prisoners refused to answer questions. The Chinese settled on a trooper of Polish origin whose relatives were potential hostages in Communist Poland. He was thoroughly questioned on a variety of topics of a tactical and strategic nature.

It was while they were at Suan that the prisoners received their first taste of political indoctrination. One of the officers, Lieutenant Probyn, had died and, after he had been buried, the Senior British officer, Major Ryan, was approached by a Chinese interpreter who offered his condolences. He went on to say that such deaths were unnecessary, but would soon cease to occur, as it was the intention and desire of the peoples of China and Russia to liberate the oppressed people of the United States and the British Commonwealth. Ryan maintained a chilling silence and walked away. Soon afterwards the prisoners were issued with letter-cards and were told to write home. They all took the opportunity to do so. It was not until they were repatriated that they discovered that not a single card had reached the United Kingdom. The information they had given was used to verify their addresses in the dossiers that the Chinese were compiling on every one of the prisoners.

The prisoners were about to learn the nature of the 'Lenient Policy' of the Chinese People's Volunteers. They were told that they were war criminals because they had fought in a war of aggression and that under the terms of the Potsdam Agreement the Chinese had the right to execute them summarily for their crimes. However, the Chinese People's

Volunteers had a policy of leniency and would not exercise their right under international law because they appreciated that the prisoners had been misled and duped by their capitalist masters. So long as the prisoners showed themselves to be willing to learn the truth the Chinese People's Volunteers would treat them leniently and would forego their rights. This argument was to be drummed into the prisoners at every opportunity, a Sword of Damocles suspended over their heads throughout captivity, and would only be set aside if the prisoners changed their attitudes and demonstrated the change by active co-operation. The Lenient Policy having been described with considerable care, the prisoners were now compelled to listen to their first political lectures. The first topic was "Capitalist Aggression in Korea". They were told that South Korea had started the war and that when it became clear that the North Koreans were more than a match for the aggressors America forced the United Nations to intervene by threatening to withdraw economic support from those nations that failed to follow her example. The reluctance of other nations was amply illustrated, the Chinese argued, by the meagre number of troops they sent into the fight. This suited the Americans who did not really seek the active participation of other nations, because all they wanted was official backing for their own aggression. Churchill had thrown in more troops than other nations because he wanted to ingratiate himself with Truman in order to get more Marshall Aid to cover budget deficiencies caused by blunders of his administration.

It seems to have escaped the notice of the Chinese propagandists that it was Clement Attlee and the Socialist Government that had ordered British troops to Korea.

The prisoners at Suan suffered several lectures on this theme. Many more awaited them in the next two and a half years at their destination and was to be repeated so often that some of it was bound to stick. In February 1951, however, these arguments were regarded by the prisoners as so much political clap-trap, so evidently crude propaganda that it was self-defeating. The time was to come when enemy censorship robbed the prisoners of news of the outside world so that they had no means of verifying much of what they were told and could not distinguish fact from blatant propaganda.

On 16 or 17 February, or thereabouts, the column prepared to leave Suan on the next stage of their march northwards. Two weeks at the Bean Camp had resulted in many deaths and had seriously weakened the underfed survivors who were now in a poor condition for marching long distances. Before they left they were asked if they felt fit enough to proceed and many of the sick and wounded were left behind. Of these Sergeant S. Rankin, Lance Corporal Harris, Gunner Slade and two Riflemen, Griffiths and Atkid, had very unexpected and remarkable luck. They and all the other p.o.w. were unaware that an important feature of the original Lenient Policy was to send a few prisoners back across the battle-field loaded with propaganda leaflets calling on the enemy troops to surrender. Thus did they regain their freedom and provide our military authorities with the first concrete evidence of how the North Koreans and Chinese were treating British p.o.w.

The unfortunate majority set off on another long march. At one stage they were promised that they would be put aboard trains, but it proved to be an idle rumour. Massey writes:–

Marching again tonight. Don't know where.
Supposed to have got a train tonight but something went wrong.
Have to march another three days.
Tonight's march nearly creased me.
Came to a little village. Slept with some Yanks and Turks.

After two days they reached Soktal-li, another mining village a few miles outside Pyongyang. Here they received a visit from a North Korean colonel, Colonel Kim, who ran an indoctrination school nearby. This school was directly supervised by his namesake, General Kim of the P.O.W. Administration. With the consent of the Chinese guards, he approached two small groups of British prisoners and delivered them a lecture on the subject of 'Peace'. He then invited them to go with him to the 'Peace Fighters' Camp'. The response was an ominous silence. Kim next turned his attention to one of the officers, an Irish Captain of the Royal Artillery, A.H.C. Gibbon, affectionately known as 'Spud' to his brother officers. He repeated his invitation and when he was politely told what he could do with his Peace Fighters' School he detailed Gibbon, Sergeant Kavanagh and a number of junior ranks to follow him into Pyongyang. The latter included a soldier who was already a card-carrying member of the British Communist Party, two members of the Young Communist League and two fellow-travellers. This party was marched into Pyongyang where many of them were so badly treated that some of them died. Those who 'volunteered' for the Peace Fighters' Camp and survived were handed back to the Chinese a year later.

The rest of the prisoners, after a brief rest, continued their northward march, passing through the western suburbs of Pyongyang. Many more fell by the wayside where they died uncomplainingly in the snow with the Chinese guards standing over them blaspheming and urging them to get up with the toes of their boots and rifle butts. The prisoners at the tail end of the column, under abuse and threats from their guards, buried the dead, though the Chinese tried to prevent them from doing so with Christian rites. The S.B.O. ignored the cocked rifles and threats to shoot him if he held burial services and insisted upon saying a few prayers each time a prisoner was lowered into a grave.

Towards the end of February the Chinese considered that the column was now far enough north for the prisoners to light fires in comparative safety. But this concession was offset by a cut in their meagre rations, if and when the guards managed to find them any food. They still had to find shelter wherever they could each night, often in derelict huts, bunkers, caves and ditches.

The precise number of p.o.w., which included more American than British, who died during this last and longest phase of the march which carried them beyond the Chongch'on River into the mountains is not known. The entire journey had been made in bitter weather, through rain, snow and ice, and many of the prisoners were wounded and frost-bitten and all were now diseased and undernourished. Massey wrote:-

Raining all day. Lucky we got a place to sleep.
23 Feb. Feeling very bad on the march. Have a cold on my chest.
This march is only supposed to last a few more days. Hope I make it.

American reports estimated that twenty per cent had died, but there is no sure way of assessing how many of the British prisoners were included in this figure. The Communists blamed these casualties on the prisoners themselves, accusing them of carrying vermin and venereal diseases into captivity. The prisoners were told that the carrying of filthy pictures and the wearing of tattoos of naked women were signs of immorality and that prisoners had died because the Americans had bombed non-military targets and so stopped medical aid and other essential supplies. When, ultimately, the Chinese authorities notified the British of the names of some of those who had died, not a single one was listed as having died of venereal disease or being the victims of American bombing or strafing. Indeed, the diseases notified were a damning indictment of neglect and starvation. They included erysipelas, dysentery, pneumonia, pellagra, tuberculosis and beri-beri.

The column reached its destination, a derelict village on the Pyoktong peninsula, on 6 March, after two months of exposure and hardship. It had taken a heavy toll of the British prisoners of whom a mere sixty had survived, including five officers out of the three hundred or so who had been captured when Seoul was over-run. The remainder had died or had been siphoned off by the North Koreans. Massey wrote:–

6th March. Arrived at our destination. Just a bombed village. Got no food here. Quite a few Yanks die here every day.
Got an overcoat and a blanket. Food not good. Sugar ration today only one spoonful each. Our food ration is 200 gms of rice per day 200 gms of millet and 200 of corn.

The camp originally designated Camp 3 was to become known as Camp 5. It was also to become the headquarters of General Wang Yang Kung of the Chinese P.O.W. Administration. In March, however, it was guarded by North Korean troops and already contained about three hundred Americans whose deplorable condition indicated what lay in store for the new arrivals. One of the first sights that the British prisoners saw was four scarecrow Americans carrying their dead comrade to the cemetery on a makeshift litter.

As the U.S authorities have freely admitted, the morale of the Americans in the camp was extremely low. Discipline had broken down almost completely and individual prisoners had little compassion for their less fortunate companions. They ignored their officers and made few organized attempts to help themselves. It fell largely to the British officers, particularly the SBO, Major Ryan, to restore some semblance of order and discipline and to organize self-help wherever possible.

4

THE KANGDONG
CAVES AND THE PEACE
FIGHTERS OF
PYONGYANG

(Camps 9 & 12)

Of the many camps, centres, bunkers, tunnels, caves and holes in the
Pyongyang area to which the North Koreans took numerous individual
prisoners and splinter groups in 1951 there were three in particular that
were to have, in their respective ways, far-reaching influences on the
subsequent behaviour of the p.o.w. These were the Kangdong Caves,
the Peace Fighters' School and the military interrogation centre known
as Pak's Palace. There was a fourth organization operating in the
Pyongyang area into the hands of which fell a few diplomatic and military
prisoners of special interest to the Russians. This was the North Korean
Security Police, the equivalent of the Soviet MVD.

The Kangdong Caves were, as the name indicates, a series of caves and
tunnels in the side of hills in the outer suburbs of Pyongyang and constituted the main North Korean p.o.w. camp in the area. Officially
designated Camp No.9, the larger caverns were grossly overcrowded, rat-
infested holes dripping with water where the prisoners struggled to survive
in darkness and their own filth; only those near the stockade doors saw
chinks of light and breathed occasional draughts of fresh air. Some of the
caves were no more than small crevices in the rocks where one man had
to lie on the damp earth drenched by the dripping water. The permanent
residents of these filthy holes were South Koreans who had been left there
to rot for months, and in some cases for years, without trial. Many groups
of British, American and other U.N. prisoners passed through this camp
en route to the Peace Fighters' School or to Pak's Palace, which also used

the caves to deposit its 'empties', i.e. people who had been interrogated, to await disposal. Some of the officers who stayed in this camp calculated that over two hundred and fifty American, British, French and other European p.o.w. died there. Conditions were so bad that prisoners would do almost anything to get out of the place, a fact well understood by the North Koreans who exploited it to force many prisoners to 'volunteer' for the Peace Fight.

The number of 'Peace Fighters' recruited in this manner was sixty. Forty of these were Americans, eighteen were British, two were Australians and one was a Turk. Just how the latter arrived there nobody seemed to know, and since he could not speak English, Chinese, Russian or Korean his part in the proceedings is of little consequence. The American contingent, led by a U.S. Army Colonel who had been recruited by Colonel Kim in the winter of 1950, was already installed in a battered school in the south-eastern suburbs of the city when the first batch of British prisoners arrived in March 1951.

The circumstances in which the British party was recruited later became the subject of a special enquiry as a result of a Parliamentary Question tabled in 1955 about the death of one of the party, Sergeant L. Kavanagh.

The story begins at the transit camp at Soktal-li, the Mining Camp, on about 20 February. As mentioned in the previous chapter, Colonel Kim selected sixteen prisoners, including Captain Gibbon, Sergeant Kavanagh, Sergeant Nugent, who had a head wound, three other sergeants and ten Other Ranks, including a member of the British Communist Party (who shall be called 'Comrade'), to follow him into Pyongyang. He marched them into the suburbs where they were quartered in a dirty barrack hut where there were already ten American p.o.w. Kim once again invited all the prisoners to go with him to a school in the city where, he said, there were already twenty Americans avidly studying the 'truth'. When they had learned it they would be released to their own lines. He hinted that none of these 'students' wished to return to the deplorable conditions of the camps they had previously been in and he promised the new recruits that they would receive decent treatment if they did as he suggested. He then asked Captain Gibbon for his views on these proposals. Gibbon refused to have anything to do with the scheme and warned his subordinates not to commit themselves to it or sign anything resembling propaganda. He left the room with Kim hard on his heels, leaving the remainder to discuss their position. They all agreed that they would do nothing improper from the military point of view, which left some of them with plenty of scope to sidle out of their agreement by participating in political activities.

The following morning Captain Gibbon, Sergeant Kavanagh, another sergeant, a corporal, a rifleman and Comrade were marched to a house in the city where they were greeted by three Chinese, several North Koreans and a British subject dressed in Chinese army winter clothing. The latter was in fact a free-lance reporter for the British Communist Party newspaper, *The Daily Worker*. He told the group that they had been brought to the house as a result of his request to meet some British p.o.w. He did not identify himself. Presumably he exchanged a few words with the prisoners before they were removed back to the barrack hut to join the others. That night the Americans in the adjacent room made a hole in the wall and after greetings discussed the days events. It transpired that they already knew of the British reporter and told the British prisoners that he had visited American p.o.w. in a camp known as 'Death Valley' where he had called them "warmongering dogs who deserved to die like dogs" and accused them of trying to change the Korean peoples' way of life. The Americans said that he was armed with a revolver when he made his speech and that later he prompted a few American prisoners in writing a propaganda leaflet which was subsequently published under the title of "P.W's. Calling". It was distributed among the U.N. troops in South Korea and around the world.

That same night Comrade was called out of the room and taken to meet the correspondent again. He was promised that he would be given D.D.T., cigarettes and matches for his companions and would arrange for them to be sent books and have shaves and haircuts. These promises were never fulfilled, but he gave Comrade some tobacco and later had the British prisoners sent a few old copies of the *Shanghai News*, a Chinese newspaper in the English language.

Evidently other exchanges took place at this nefarious interview. Comrade still possessed his party membership card and had bragged to his fellow prisoners that he would use it to gain preferential treatment. He is believed to have discovered the identity of the war correspondent, but did not reveal it to Captain Gibbon or to any of the others. He said little about what had happened on his return, except that he had been promised a few amenities.

Next day Gibbon was summoned to meet the correspondent and challenged him to identify himself and explain what he was doing behind enemy lines. The journalist declined and would only say that he was a free-lance reporter who had been in Russia and China and had just arrived in Korea. He wished to write a piece in which he could state that he had met some British officers and rankers who were astonished at the devastation caused by U.N. bombing of Pyongyang and were disgusted that hospitals and non-military targets had been bombed. Gibbon is believed to have lost his Irish temper and the interview developed into a stormy argument.

Afterwards the correspondent individually interviewed five O.Rs who Gibbon had previously warned of the journalist's proposals. These interviews were attended by North Korean officers and lasted only a few minutes. Their interview with Comrade lasted half an hour.

Later Sergeant Kavanagh foolishly confided to Comrade that, despite the presence of the North Korean officers he had threatened to strangle the reporter if he could get his hands round his scrawny neck and the journalist responded by threatening to have him shot. From here on Kavanagh was a marked man.

The following day the British prisoners, including Comrade, were consigned to the Kangdong Caves. Kavanagh was already suffering from dysentery and the early symptoms of beri-beri. They shared the filthy accommodation with fifty or sixty South Koreans living in dreadful squalor and for the next two weeks they were not allowed to wash or to take any exercise. They were fed a small bowl of corn twice daily and were refused medical attention. They were joined by a party of recently captured Americans, some of whom were seriously wounded but had received no medical attention.

On 7 March, or thereabouts, Comrade and a Rifleman were transferred to the Peace Fighters' School. Subsequently Comrade was sent back to the Caves to try and persuade the others to follow his example. Three days later Captain Gibbon and the wounded Sergeant Nugent were collected by a North Korean intelligence officer, Colonel Lee, and taken to Pak's Palace for interrogation. Gibbon was brutally tortured for refusing to give information about an escape attempt which he had helped to arrange. His hands were tied behind his back and he was hung from a tree and beaten and kicked for many hours before being cut down. On repatriation he was awarded the George Medal for refusing to reveal the route which the escapers had taken. Sergeant Nugent was beaten and eventually sent back to a transit camp, probably the Bean Camp where he eventually died of his unattended wounds and diseases on 25 April 1951.

Sergeant Kavanagh and Corporal Davidson were left to rot in the Kangdong Caves and after an unknown period were transferred to the Bean Camp at Suan. Kavanagh, a very sick man, was denied food and medical attention for refusing to participate in propaganda activities. He was returned to the Chinese who sent him to Soktal-li, the Mining Camp, where he died on 4 September.

Corporal Davidson, also a very sick man, was also returned to the Chinese and was marched with one of the April evacuation columns to Camp No 1 at Chongsong, where he died of beri-beri shortly afterwards.

It will be seen from this that the chances of surviving imprisonment in the Caves was small. The place was a death trap with three exits, the Bean Camp and subsequent death from neglect, Pak's Palace, torture and probable death from ill treatment, or a chance of survival by 'volunteering' for the Peace Fighters' School. It is scarcely surprising that many prisoners chose the latter.

Of the original sixteen prisoners who had been rounded up by Colonel Kim, ten chose the School. Four died in miserable conditions, one, Captain Gibbon, survived after torture, and one, Sergeant O'Hara survived being returned to the transit camps.

The North Koreans lost little time in putting the new 'Peace Fighters' to work producing political propaganda. They produced a pamphlet called 'May We be Heard' which was distributed among the British p.o.w. captured in April.

The next group of British prisoners to be routed towards the Peace Fighters' School was a party of about eighteen sick and wounded captured after the Imjin River battle. Their senior was Lieutenant Terry Waters of the West Yorkshire Regiment, a young officer recently out of Sandhurst seconded to the Glosters. He was suffering from a serious head wound and a wound in an arm. He and his party were incarcerated in the Caves for the better part of a month, by which time they were starving. Their companions were South Koreans, Americans and other U.N. prisoners who were in rags, filthy and crawling with lice and were daily dying in considerable numbers. Colonel Kim paid them a visit to urge them to join the Peace Fighters. They held out for as long as they could, but it became obvious that unless they accepted the offer they would soon all die. Waters ordered his subordinates to accept the offer but refused it himself despite repeated attempts by Colonel Kim and his men to persuade him to join the party. He died soon afterwards and after the war was posthumously awarded the George Cross.

Not all of this party reached the Peace Fighters' School. Some of them were snaffled by the Chinese for their own propaganda offensive. But those who reached the School were compelled to participate actively in the 'Fight for Peace', and some of them were convinced of the Communist cause and later were used to indoctrinate their fellow p.o.w.

The Peace Fighters spent a year in Pyongyang and were subjected to an intensive course not only of political re-education but also in the Communists' party organization and procedures. They were promised early release if they reached a satisfactory standard and were threatened with a return to the Caves if they failed. Very few failed.

The course comprised endless lectures and discussions on the Communist version of world history, economics, sociology and American 'aggression'. They were also compelled to set up study groups led by American officers for the study of selected pieces of literature, art, music and handicrafts. Among the classics they were obliged to study were the works of Dickens, which, their captors insisted, depicted life and the social evils of twentieth century Britain. They also had to study the works of Theodore Dreiser and translations of heavy Russian political tomes. Perhaps of more immediate utility were the lessons they were given on how to run their daily lives on Communist lines, how to organize 'democratic' elections and run political groups and leisure activities. In the process they learned some sharp practices like using lists containing only officially approved candidates for elections, or counterbalancing genuinely democratically elected committees by co-opting an equal number of ex-officio, officially approved members and giving them powers of vote. Translated into action in the Yalu River p.o.w. camps at a later date, it meant that the prisoners' truly democratically elected representatives could be easily neutralized.

Some of the earlier Peace Fighters were taken into Pyongyang shortly after it had been bombed by U.N. aircraft. They were led among the smouldering ruins and shown bomb-blasted corpses of women and children, and children crying over the corpses of their parents. They were told that the beautiful city was an 'open' city with no military value. Yet not half a mile away across the Taedong River which runs through the centre of the capital, their fellow U.N. prisoners of war, some of them British, were being forced to work in slave labour gangs in warehouses, supply dumps and marshalling yards shifting war materials that were being dispersed among domestic dwellings. The capital was littered with military establishments; troops were billeted in the houses and in one built-up area the houses had been bulldozed on either side of a main road to make an airstrip.

The criticism that was aimed at the U.N. aircraft, especially the United States aircraft, for their alleged indiscriminate bombing of dwellings ignored the fact that throughout the Communist-occupied parts of the country ordinary dwellings were used to billet troops and to store military supplies, because all the military supply depots and warehouses had been reduced to rubble. Many British and American p.o.w. reported after their repatriation that every village they passed through during the evacuation period, or subsequently during escape attempts, had under its roofs either troops, military supplies or both, in addition to housing the civilian population.

Most of the Peace Fighters were allowed, indeed were compelled, to read translations of supposedly genuine documents which their captors claimed 'proved' that the war had been started by the South Koreans with American connivance. The originals were supposed to have been captured in Seoul from the South Korean Government archives and had been subsequently lodged with the United Nations. The following example was supposedly written by the South Korean President Syngman Rhee to somebody in the U.S. Government. It reads as follows, including the inverted commas round every sentence:–

"I feel strongly that now is the most psychological moment when we should take an aggressive measures." "We will all work together, you in Washington and we here in Seoul and Tokyo." "Convince the American statesmen and the general public and let them quietly agree that we go ahead and carry out our program and give us all the material we need." "The longer we drag the harder it will be."

There were many other, equally conspiratorial examples. Whether or not they were genuine is a matter of speculation, but it is known for certain that they went a long way towards convincing the Peace Fighters that the South Koreans, with American connivance, started the war and that the American intervention was 'unlawful'.

Soon after Comrade entered the Peace Fighters' School he became a leading light in its activities, primarily because his long-standing membership of the Communist Party had made him familiar with its jargon and organizational procedures. He is said to have been on fairly good terms with all the British contingent, who are alleged to have been grateful to him for getting them out of the Caves. Their gratitude was undeserved since at this stage it is very doubtful if the North Koreans cared a fig for his membership of the BCP, otherwise they would not have sent him back to the Caves for a fortnight after he had revealed his membership to them.

Comrade's greatest rivals were the American officers whose ranks and

35

superior education made them of greater literary and propaganda value. His main value was his relations with his fellow countrymen, which permitted his captors to keep themselves informed of the prisoners' genuine attitudes and political progress. In short, he was their stool pigeon. According to his captors, in May 1951 he had the bright idea of forming a 'Peace' organization and managed to persuade his fellow p.o.w., British and American, to petition the North Korean President, Kim Il Sung, for permission to set up what was grandly known as "The U.S.-British War Prisoners Peace Organization". Nothing could have been more preposterously atypical of a British soldier's spontaneous behaviour. It was comparable to some obscure British soldier in a prison camp in Germany in the Second World War, writing an appeal to Hitler for permission to start a pro-Nazi organization. Nevertheless this organization was to become a powerful propaganda weapon against the U.N. cause world-wide. Permission was granted, and according to the Communists, the idea was so enthusiastically received by the prisoners in *all* the p.o.w. camps in North Korea that they, too, sought and were granted permission to form their own Peace Committees.

Thus did the Communists launch one of their biggest propaganda stunts of the war and, backed by their world-wide propaganda resources, used it to try and convince the entire world that the U.S.-British War Prisoners Peace Organization was a democratically elected body speaking on behalf of *all* p.o.w. Also that *all* the p.o.w. in their hands condemned the American and South Korean aggressors and passionately desired peace on their terms.

The truth was that the fifty-eight Peace Fighters represented a mere 1.2% of the British and American p.o.w., the vast majority of whom were held by the Chinese in the Yalu River camps over two hundred miles to the north of Pyongyang and they had not had any contact with the Pyongyang rabble. Therefore they had never been given an opportunity to elect the officers of the US-British War Prisoners Peace Organization. In any case its officers had been foisted into office by rigged elections at the Peace Fighters' School.

Although the idea was supposedly that of Comrade, who was initially made its President, he was demoted to the role of Vice-President after 'democratic' elections had bestowed the Presidency on an American Captain. Comrade is known to have been hurt by his defeat which, as he saw it, was a defeat for the proletariat.

When, eventually, Peace Committees were formed in the Chinese-controlled p.o.w. camps, the Presidents were all American officers, despite the fact that most of the people nominated for the office were enlisted men!

The election of officers for the Central Committee of the US-British War Prisoners Peace Organization was followed by 'democratic' elections of officers for a variety of sub-committees, such as the Editorial Board, the Platform Board etc. Curiously, the same clique that populated the main committee was voted into office as the senior officers of all these sub-committees. They were an American captain, an American major and Comrade.

Soon after the charade of creating the organization and electing its officers the Peace Fighters were put to work preparing material for publication and broadcasting. According to one of them, it soon became apparent that, except for the American officers, the majority lacked the literary talent necessary to produce adequate propaganda material. At first the less articulate prisoners got round this difficulty by stringing together Communist jargon copied directly out of their notebooks and textbooks. The authors of the best of these efforts were escorted either singly or in pairs into the capital to make recordings for broadcasting. Evidently the results were unconvincing. It dawned on the North Koreans that these prisoners were incapable of producing work that sounded spontaneous and authentic to the outside world. The education of the Peace Fighters was intensified. They were supplied with more books to improve their vocabularies and their use of Communist jargon. Literary and reading circles were formed to improve their written and spoken words, with Comrade acting as the tutor to the British contingent. However, his limitations became obvious and after some wrangling the American officers were formed into a literary advisory committee to take over the task. Comrade is said to have been furious and accused the Americans of trying to form a ruling clique to ingratiate themselves with their captors.

Henceforth the production of propaganda was an elaborate business. The programme planners, that is the American officers and Comrade, drafted out a monthly schedule of broadcasts and publications and submitted it to their captors for approval. If approved the better-educated Peace Fighters set to work on the manuscripts, the drafts of which were submitted to a literary advisory committee for revision. It was re-vetted by the North Koreans who handed the approved copy to prisoners selected by them to use in making speeches or broadcasts.

After the war an investigation into the activities of the Peace Fighters, their production of propaganda and the conflict between the leading American officers and Comrade, produced some interesting insights.

The senior American officer, a Colonel, claimed that he had been the victim of circumstances and had done all he could to limit the damage of the propaganda and indeed had done his best to sabotage it and sabotage the indoctrination of the Peace Fighters. Some support for his claim came from one of the principal British Peace Fighters whom I interviewed at great length when he was repatriated. According to this source Comrade's literary ineptitude provided an opportunity for the American officers to create the literary advisory committee with the intention of using it as a device for signalling to their superiors in the West that they were producing the material under duress, by peppering it with uniquely Communist jargon and producing material of such a high literary standard that when printed or spoken over the radio by ordinary soldiers it would sound suspiciously literate and patently not of their composition.

It was one of my tasks during the Korean War to keep an eye open for just this sort of thing. In a different context, a similar ruse was used to discredit their confessions of guilt by many Western victims of Communist show trials that regularly took place in all the East European Communist states at the height of the Cold War. And, as with them, Western officials took the view that the material spoken by the victims had been scripted by their interrogators and indoctrinators and not by themselves. The same interpretation was put on the propaganda broadcast by the Peace Fighters over Pyongyang radio. Consequently the intentions of the literary advisory committee failed to have the desired effect.

Relatively few broadcasts over Pyongyang radio were made in person by the Peace Fighters. Usually selected titbits of their material were read by an English-speaking commentator. The first broadcast by a British prisoner was transmitted on 11 July 1951 and was made in person by Comrade, who had recorded it three months previously. The next two were made on 23 October by a sergeant, from scripts prepared by Comrade. Most of the broadcasts were made in December 1951 and covered a variety of topics including derisive comments on the Kaesong Peace talks, belated messages to British electors (a general election was in the offing when they were prepared), commentaries on the proceedings of the US-British War Prisoners Peace Organization and passionate denials of North Korean atrocities against p.o.w. Apparently, whenever the latter appeared in the American press, a teleprinter in Pyongyang recorded the details and the tapes were rushed to the Peace Fighters who were ordered to draft suitable denials and praise their captors for their good treatment. Many of the broadcasts consisted of announcers reading extracts from the prisoners' private letters to their relatives, mail that was never forwarded to the addressees.

The culmination of many months of indoctrination of the Peace Fighters was a much-publicized convention of the US-British War Prisoners Peace Organization. The proceedings were attended by photographers and pressmen from all over the Communist bloc, including a hefty contingent from Soviet Russia. There was a day-long orgy of speech-making. The Central Committee sat on a raised platform in a large hall bedecked with peace doves and banners calling upon all p.o.w. and the world in general to condemn the American aggression and to petition for peace. The speeches of the Central Committee occupied much time. Typical of its messages is a speech made by Comrade as the Vice President of the Organization. He ranted:–

It was not by accident that we became prisoners of war. We are prisoners because we came to Korea as tools to further the designs of the warmongers and capitalists, who foment wars for their own personal mercenary designs. Nor was it by accident that, after becoming prisoners of war, we as a group, learning the true facts behind the Korean War, became strongly imbued with the desire to form a peace fighter's organization and contribute our energies, small though they may be, in the fight for a peaceful and tranquil world. We therefore desire to band ourselves together to direct our fight as a collective group in the struggle against wars, which retard progress destroy civilization and, if brazenly continued, will decimate all of mankind.

In later speeches from the platform the ringleaders tried to justify the intervention of the Chinese with a number of specious arguments. Comrade had the cheek to declaim:–

Surely if the United States has the right to 'protect' the entire Western hemisphere by military action, the Chinese Peoples' Volunteers have the right to aid their neighbour, Korea. Ninety-three percent of all the U.S. and British prisoners demand that the legal representatives of the People's Republic of China be admitted to the United Nations Organization.

Soon afterwards a 300-page report entitled *Our Fight for Peace* was issued worldwide and was distributed free of charge to delegates of the

Communist-inspired International Peace Congress which was held in Vienna. I received a copy by courtesy of the Scottish National Union of Students who sent it to the War Office out of malevolent political motives, doubtless unaware of its intelligence value.

Our Fight for Peace gives the impression that the US-British War Prisoners Peace Organization conference held by the Peace Fighters was attended on their own initiative by p.o.w. from Britain, America, South Korea, Turkey, Australia, Holland, Belgium and France. Sadly, *Our Fight for Peace* impressed a large number of well-meaning people in the Western world who remain in ignorance of how the Peace Fighters, a handful of men, recruited from the lethal misery of the Caves and isolated from the main bodies of British and American p.o.w. were ruthlessly exploited for political gain under threats of being returned thereto.

Sometime during December the Peace Fighters received a visit from the North Korean General Kim of the P.O.W Administration. He informed them that they would be repatriated, the long-promised reward that had been dangled before them at the moment of their recruitment and frequently repeated to ensure their motivation. Then came the pay-off. Before repatriation, however, the General added, they would be sent to P.O.W. Camp No. 5 at Pyoktong.

Thus were the Peace Fighters robbed of their hopes of early release. They were bundled into lorries where they were joined by other British p.o.w. who had been held in Pyongyang, including Lieutenant Guy Temple of the Glosters, who had been tortured in Pak's Palace. He had some devastating remarks to make to the sergeants among the Peace Fighters, reminding them of their responsibilities as soldiers and the penalties they would face under the Army Acts upon repatriation. With this the lorries bounced up the frozen roads on the first stages of their long journey to the Yalu River.

Upon their arrival at Camp 5, which was Chinese-controlled, they were received with indifference. The Chinese had long since set up their own organization to rival the North Korean Peace Fighters' efforts, and clearly did not want them contaminating their organization with a Russian/North Korean version. The Peace Fighters were consigned to a compound of American negro p.o.w. Comrade is said to have used his influence to get them shifted to another compound where they were actually still isolated from other prisoners in the camp. They were told that they were no longer to function as a Central Committee but must, like all the other prisoners, organize themselves into sanitation and other 'Daily Life' committees. Two of the Americans refused to accept these terms, arguing that the camp already possessed effective committees performing these functions. The Chinese argued with them for six hours before shifting all of them to another area near the camp headquarters where they were placed under armed guards. They were effectively under arrest.

Rumours spread among the prisoners in the main camp that the new arrivals were being forced to sign statements condemning the Americans for waging germ warfare on North Korea. To offset the rumours, the Chinese demanded that the former Central Committee members should all sign statements denying them and also denying that they were being held under armed guard and were being forced to remain in their billets. The Committee refused and hours were spent defining what was intended by the term 'force'. The upshot was that the defunct Central Committee 'resigned' and agreed to sign statements if, on their part, the Chinese agreed to release an American officer in the main compound who had been arrested as the alleged ringleader of a strike. The American was released, the Committee signed their statements and immediately afterwards the American officer was re-arrested and sentenced to six months' imprisonment! That was the end of the Central Committee and the fight for peace.

Situated in a brickyard in Pyongyang was the North Korean military interrogation centre, Pak's Palace, also know to the prisoners as Pak's Death House. Prisoners were brought here from numerous squalid p.o.w. 'camps' within a fifty-mile radius of the capital, including the Kangdong Caves, camps where American, British and other European p.o.w. had been held by the North Koreans for weeks in dark caverns similar to the Caves, often deprived of food and water until they agreed to answer questions or otherwise cooperate.

The makeshift character of the centre was matched by the disorganized, amateurish teams of sadistic North Korean interrogators more skilled in torment and torture than they were in asking pertinent and penetrating questions on relevant matters of military intelligence.

Whatever organization the Russians had originally created was presumably disrupted, if not mostly destroyed by MacArthur's daring offensive in the autumn of 1950. The towns and cities of North Korea, including Pyongyang, had been partially destroyed during the U.N. advance up the Korean peninsula, which had also, presumably, destroyed many of the buildings used by the North Korean military intelligence organization. Similarly, its records must have been destroyed by bombing and shelling, or captured by the U.N. forces or had been hastily removed to the north of the country. The offensive also netted 100,000 North

Koreans which must have included a significant proportion of military intelligence personnel, especially those manning the lower echelons whom, we now know, probably had less than three years' military service. In all probability the senior personnel had fled with their Russian advisers to Sinuiju and other frontier towns with easy access into the safety of Manchuria. These senior officers had been trained by the Red Army and had lived in Russia for years. Some of them could speak three languages, Korean, Russian and English, with an American accent. It is therefore not surprising that they had also picked up some of the nastier Russian interrogation routines in addition to their own traditionally cruel natures.

The consequence of all these factors was that the North Korean military p.o.w. intelligence organization was a ramshackle affair compared with that of the Chinese, seemingly run by a handful of senior officers of dubious experience and manned by a relatively small number of junior officers with very little knowledge or experience in matters of military intelligence and even less in how to organize an efficient p.o.w. intelligence agency. It will be recalled that North Korea had only come into existence five years previously and it did not possess a modern or a large Air Force or Navy and its Army was not equipped with modern weapons by Western standards. Consequently their interrogators possessed only limited and superficial knowledge of matters normally of interest to military intelligence.

There was little evidence of the existence of a field interrogation organization for picking out prisoners of intelligence interest from the prisoners in the evacuation columns. Pak's Palace, as we have seen, drew its prisoners seemingly randomly from filthy transit camps like the Kangdong Caves, mostly the sick and wounded who had the misfortune to be left behind in the winter and spring of 1951 when their fitter comrades were taken north by the Chinese. Prisoners of particular intelligence interest, like diplomats, very senior officers such as the American General Dean and many airmen, were snaffled by the Security Police, the North Korean equivalent to the Soviet MVD, which had precedence over the army and the Political Bureau commissars in the selection of suitable victims. The commissars in turn, as we have seen, also seem to have had precedence over the Army for choice of prisoners.

According to several British p.o.w., including Pilot R.H. Johnson of the Fleet Air Arm, conditions in the brickyard, although deplorable, were better than those in the outlying feeder camps. Once in Pak's Palace, the sick or wounded, already much debilitated by their detention in the awful transit camps, were required to work while awaiting interrogation or between periods of questioning. They were given back-breaking tasks such as cutting and hauling timber and filthy jobs like cleaning out the Korean latrines, earthenware jars sunk into the ground, with their bare hands. They were never allowed to wash afterwards and had to clean themselves as best they could with dirt or on their own clothing. This was a job the North Koreans delighted in giving to officer-prisoners. Some prisoners were sent to weed nearby fields or to muck out cattle stalls and some were dispatched to military supply points to load or unload ammunition and combustibles from trains and lorries, often during air raids. Using prisoners for forced labour was a typically Russian habit in this period of history.

Under the circumstances it is not surprising that Pak's Palace was regarded as a death camp since a high proportion of the prisoners sent there died during their stay or shortly after leaving, of diseases or their wounds or from neglect and from physical abuse under questioning.

By November 1952 the terrible 'feeder' camps serving the centre appear to have closed, or nearly so, either because the inmates had died or because they had been transferred into Chinese custody and sent north to the camps on the Yalu River. Thereafter teams of North Koreans trawled through the Chinese-controlled camps for prisoners, usually officers, to take back to Pak's Palace for interrogation on military matters.

Ostensibly the interrogation centre was run by the North Korean army but eyewitness reports and expert analysis of their questions, techniques and procedures left little doubt that they were aided by, advised and loosely supervised by a group of Russians under the command of Colonel Andrep of the MVD from a building three-quarters of a mile away. The principal Korean army interrogator at Pak's Palace was originally Colonel Lee, a multi-lingual character who in May 1951 contracted pleurisy and had to surrender his command to the notorious Major Pak, after whom the centre gained its name. The bucolic Colonel Lee had long been suffering from a leg wound which he received while improving his marksmanship on a small canister which turned out to be an American anti-personnel butterfly bomb. After he left, conditions in the brickyard deteriorated markedly. Rations were cut and harsher punishments were meted out for petty infractions.

The selection of prisoners for interrogation was extremely crude and patently lacked even elementary objectivity. No attempt seems to have been made to match the level or value of the knowledge likely to be held by prisoners with the capabilities of the interrogators. The onus of judging what information might be of intelligence value was often placed squarely on the unfortunate prisoners who were beaten up if what they had to say displeased their questioners. Officers of the rank of colonel were used to question prisoners for tactical information that would have been dealt with by sergeants in field interrogation teams in any Western system. Where the target of the interrogation was specified it was often something which the victim did not in any case possess.

Soviet intervention could easily be deduced from a sudden relevant burst of questions from a previously incompetent North Korean and from changes in style of the interrogator. The latter's inability spontaneously to evaluate the information would turn to wrath after he had consulted somebody behind the scenes. But more objective indications of Soviet intervention were the eye-witness reports of p.o.w. who were questioned by Russians.

The active participation of the Russians in the affairs of Pak's Palace became evident early in February 1951. Their first known Commonwealth victim was Flight Lieutenant G.R. Harvey of the Royal Australian Air Force, after he had been beaten up by Colonel Lee and Major Pak. Unable to obtain from him whatever information they were seeking, Lee took him before a European-looking individual dressed in civvies. Lee acted as interpreter for questioning which took place in three languages. However, he evidently was unable to cope and the exasperated civilian addressed Harvey directly in fluent English and proceeded to question him in an expert and knowledgeable fashion on air intelligence matters.

Rifleman Clifford was also questioned in fluent English by a European-looking civilian during this period and in this instance his interrogator stated that he was Russian. In May Private A.A. Marsh, MM, a Glosters sniper, and others of his party were also questioned in fluent English by a civilian whom they believed was a Russian.

In the late summer a party of three Russians, two of them dressed in civvies, the third wearing a uniform without badges, paid a sudden visit to the brickyard. At their approach the North Koreans hustled their prisoners into their quarters, but overlooked two who were working at a well. One of these was Guy Temple, a Russian-speaking officer of the Glosters, who managed to have a long talk with the visitors in their own language. The Russian in uniform was the leader of the trio and was anxious to get his civilian fellow countrymen to leave. They are believed to have been newspaper reporters.

Although there is only one known instance of a Russian interrogator beating up a British prisoner, a private of the Glosters, there were several recorded instances of them allowing, or ordering Lee or Pak or their henchmen to use violent methods. A Russian was present when Captain Gibbon was being tortured by Pak who made a vicious attack upon the most sensitive part of the male anatomy.

A Fleet Air Arm pilot and Australian and South African pilots reported that their North Korean interrogators selected their questions from books which listed a large number of technical questions which only the Russians would have had the knowledge to compile. The pilots soon discovered that they could hoodwink their interrogators with fanciful rubbish, except that when it was evaluated, almost certainly by Russian collators, the consequences could be a sound beating, or worse. They were also beaten for failing to answer utterly preposterous questions such as those about the type of coding systems used by the Secret Services, the strategic deployment of air forces and other matters to which only civilian intelligence officers or very senior staff officers might be privy.

After the transfer of most of the prisoners to Chinese custody Major Pak and his thugs travelled up to the Yalu River camps in search of more victims. At this point in time any tactical information the prisoners may have possessed would have been thoroughly out of date. It is therefore tempting to conclude that the Russians must have realized the inadequacy of the information gained from indiscriminate interrogation of the streams of prisoners passing through North Korean transit camps and were out to repair the situation by selective re-examination of prisoners, mostly officers.

The most important rival organization to Pak's ramshackle outfit was the North Korean Security Police, commanded by Lieutenant-General Pang Ha Sae. It had a countrywide network of police stations and interrogation centres stretching from the 38th Parallel to the Manchurian frontier. They also possessed a chain of prisons, not of the makeshift kind used by the military, but properly constructed cell blocks and equipped with torture chambers. From information provided by escapers such as Farrar-Hockley it seems that this organization was regionalized, that each regional H.Q. acted as though it was autonomous from the central heaquarters located in a concrete building in the centre of Pyongyang. The interrogation centre in the capital seems to have been a collecting centre as well as a detailed interrogation centre for special categories of p.o.w., including the most senior American p.o.w., General Dean. Others passed through en route to or out of another centre at Sinuiju, in the extreme north-west corner of the country on the border with Manchuria with easy access across the Yalu River to the Manchurian town of Antung. Another important regional centre was situated at Man po, another border town.

45

The Russians are known to have had a presence in Man po, Sinuiju and especially in Antung through which selected prisoners, especially aircrew were routed to prisons in Mukden, the provincial capital of Manchuria.

Captain Farrar-Hockley, the Adjutant of the Glosters, after several escape attempts, was eventually to find himself a guest in the police headquarters in Sinuiju where he was flung into a cell block containing Korean political prisoners and kept there for fifteen days. Although he does not record what happened to him there, it is possible that he was suspected of being a secret agent because of his many escape attempts and was being assessed for his usefulness as a source to the Russians. Some American Air Force personnel are believed to have been taken into Russia from here for detailed interrogation and were never seen again. Long after the war information from former Russian prisoners of a slave labour camp strongly suggested that these men, after years of torment and interrogation, were dumped and lost in the Gulag Archipelago.

After his sojourn in Sinuiju Farrar-Hockley was sent back to the Pyongyang secret police headquarters where he was housed in a barn and made to work cleaning latrines and cattle stalls. He escaped with two others but was recaptured and subsequently subjected to horrific torture for refusing to tell his tormentors the direction his fellow escapers had taken. He was dragged into a torture chamber and tied to a chair which was kicked over on to its back. A cloth was then thrown over his face and mouth and splashed with water repeatedly until he began to suffocate. More water was added until he lost consciousness. They revived him by applying cigarettes to his bare flesh. He was also severely beaten, cracking two of his ribs and bruising him from head to foot. His torturers kept this up for the better part of a week, during which he was given little to eat and nothing to drink. Soon he was so weak that he was barely conscious.

By this time the other two escapers had been caught and had been badly beaten into 'confessing' to the error of their ways. They were told they would be taken out and shot but were released into the custody of the North Korean army and were dumped in the Kandong Caves only to be tormented by Colonel Kim and his propagandists. From the Caves a party of very sick British, Commonwealth and American prisoners, including Farrar-Hockley, accompanied by a cart to carry those too sick to walk, were forced to march two hundred miles north to the Yalu River in bitter winter weather and snowstorms. Many of them died before they reached their destination, a modestly equipped 'hospital' run by the Chinese, who, to their credit, did what they could to clean up the ragged prisoners, issued them with warm clothing, fed them and tried to nurse them back to health.

But their help came too late and one by one many of the survivors of the march died. By incredible strength of will Farrar-Hockley survived, but was discharged before he had fully recovered for refusing to sign a statement praising the Chinese for their kind treatment. He was sent to the nearby p.o.w. camp at Pyoktong where he was reunited with members of his regiment.

5

THE KANGGYE
EXPERIMENT

(Camp 10)

The first United Nations prisoners to be taken by the Chinese were two hundred and fifty Americans and twenty-five British marines. They were ambushed at Koto-ri on 30 November 1950 while fighting a rearguard action to allow other United Nations units, principally South Koreans, to withdraw by sea through the port of Hungnam in the far north-east of the country.

After capture, the marines were quickly evacuated across seventy miles of snow-covered mountains to Kanggye where the Chinese set up their first p.o.w. camp, later known as camp 10. They were the first English-speaking troops ever to fall into the hands of the Chinese Communists, who immediately applied their original Lenient Policy, which had, of course, been designed for use on Chinese peasant soldiery.

The British and Americans were not in fact the first Westerners to experience the Lenient Policy. A few months earlier about ten German deserters from the French Foreign Legion had surrendered to the Viet-Minh in Indo-China and had been smuggled into China where they were imprisoned with Red Army defaulters for the purpose of re-education.

But, as captured Chinese documents subsequently confirmed, the treatment of the marines during their three months at Kanggye was an experiment which resulted in the modification of various aspects of the original Lenient Policy. The Kanggye experiment is of particular interest because the Royal Marines who were taken there suffered the highest death rate of any British unit in captivity and produced the highest percentage of prisoners who actively collaborated with their captors. The latter were led by a marine with an engaging personality, militant political opinions and natural powers of leadership. His name was Andrew Condron and he was the only British p.o.w. to refuse repatriation at the end of the war. He was to rise to the most influential position in the organization imposed upon the prisoners by the Chinese once they reached the permanent p.o.w. camps.

In the Koto-ri ambush the marines had acquitted themselves in the highest traditions of their Corps; they fought quite literally to the last round of ammunition and lost all their officers and senior NCOs and many of the men taken prisoner were wounded, some mortally. Condron fought gallantly and indeed made an attempt to help his mates to get away by remaining in a ditch to give them a murderous covering fire with an automatic weapon. Five corporals, nineteen marines and a severely wounded Navy Sick Berth Attendant were captured alive, though some of them died shortly afterwards. The survivors were very young and most of them had joined the Corps on long-term contracts straight from school a year or two before entering combat. Robbed of their officers and elders, they were without suitable experience to guide them in captivity but a natural leader emerged, Marine P.D. Murphy.

Soon after capture they were able to get together to decide what they should do and one of their first decisions was to invent a suitable cover story for one of their number who was a member of their unit's Intelligence section. Despite all that happened subsequently, this man was never betrayed, not even by Condron.

The Chinese lost no time in sorting out their prisoners and, in contrast to their disorganization five months later, the interrogation of them was both efficient and timely. The marines were disarmed and thoroughly searched and their unit was identified by the simple process of removing a corporal's cap badge and comparing it with a chart containing pictures of British unit badges and insignia. It was a small but significant indication of the preparedness of the Chinese Peoples' 'Volunteers' and it soon became apparent that they were already aware of the names, ranks and functions of many of the officers of the 41st Independent Commando Brigade and had similar details of the officers of the 3nd Royal Marines Commando Brigade which at this time was operating in Malaya. Two of the marines were segregated for more detailed interrogation and they were not seen again for many months. The main party was sent with the Americans to Kanggye.

Life at Kanggye was completely unexpected. The p.o.w. anticipated that they would be as brutally treated as prisoners of the North Koreans had been. The highly political character of the Chinese Lenient Policy was completely unheard of and it was a shock to be sent to school to learn politics. Although their accommodation was primitive and bitterly cold, their food grossly inadequate and their wounds remained unattended, they were compelled to attend political lectures and discussion groups. Prisoners who declined to participate were not at first brutally treated but were regarded as wayward children. They were scolded and reasoned with and if this failed they suddenly found themselves short of rations, such as they were.

Soon after reaching Kanggye the p.o.w. were issued with a questionnaire described as a P.O.W. Registration Card. It was eleven inches square and was a primitive autobiographical inventory, hand-written on cyclostyled paper of poor quality. It was ruled into sections. On the left-hand side were questions about the prisoner's private affairs, including his nationality, education, occupation in civil life, pay, marital status and political beliefs. Below this were similar questions about their wives and close relatives. Each section contained a box marked 'Property'.

Complacently smiling young Chinese Political Officers moved among the prisoners as they pored over these bewildering questionnaires, helping them to complete the questions, urging them to put in the boxes marked 'property' the number of poultry and livestock which they or their relatives possessed! The prisoners were severely admonished when they listed cars, motor cycles, houses and furniture and were called liars by the infuriated Chinese who insisted that they *must* possess livestock. How could the downtrodden, duped tools of feudal Western capitalism possess material riches? They utterly refused to believe that their prisoners were not feudal peasants.

A captured Chinese document of a later period gave detailed instructions to Political and Intelligence officers telling them how to handle American p.o.w. Various remarks made in it suggest that it was based upon their experience at Kanggye and confirmed their lack of experience in handling Western p.o.w. Dated 20 March 1951, it was written by a high-ranking Chinese officer on the basis of their interrogation of a sample of fifty Americans. It ran:–

To interrogate American prisoners is a new kind of task which we have never encountered before. Therefore we have been handicapped by our own insufficient knowledge about their character and ways of thinking. However, we have gained some experience during the past four months. The following is presented as a guide.

There followed some trite remarks about what sort of preparations interrogators should make and then continued:–

Explain first our traditional good treatment of prisoners to remove their fears and mental obstacles. Then, if possible, try to make them comprehend a few important questions (such as the meaning of wars etc). Try to convince them we are right. Break their self-conceitedness. Thus we can get more understanding of the prisoners and make out further methods and manner of handling them.

It continues:–

P.W.s will be brought together to discuss political problems. Material should be well prepared and care must be taken to maintain order.

Then come instructions on how to interrogate:–

To interrogate these prisoners who are relatively stubborn, reactive and wicked, we should adopt special interrogation methods. . . . Basic characteristics of American prisoners are fear of death; home-sickness; tiredness of war; not knowing why they should fight in Korea. They are forced and cheated to come to Korea. Their minds are deeply poisoned by reactive propaganda. P.W. can be divided into the following types.

Progressive types: Mostly youthful soldiers. They sympathize with our thinking. They are willing to talk. To them we should give encouragement and education. They should be treated very well so that they work for us and give us information of real value.

Timid Doubtful types: They usually don't want to speak too much and would try to avoid important questions. They are afraid of death. The best way to deal with them is to grasp their weakness and force them to be obedient by torturing them.

Very Stubborn Ones. They would say they know nothing, but actually they are afraid of death and are homesick. We should treat them severely from the beginning, torture them and lock them up for several days to cause them mental conflict. Assign someone to watch their reactions, then change interrogators and interrogate them all over again.

Stupid Uneducated Ones: We can only get their unit designations and their daily activities. Don't waste time on them, but be sure you are not fooled.

The document ends on a curiously paradoxical note in view of the orders to torture:–

> Truly carry out our policy of treating prisoners kindly. This will give the prisoners a good impression and make them easy to handle afterwards. Education of prisoners has proved to be very effective. But our manners and ways should be such as to make the prisoners respect and fear at the same time.

Despite the references to torture, as far as is known none of the British p.o.w. at Kanggye was tortured or witnessed other prisoners being tortured. On the whole their treatment followed precisely the instructions given in this document. In addition, they were promised that if they showed sufficient 'progress' they would be released and in due course nineteen of them were sent back through the front lines, loaded with propaganda leaflets, the largest number to be repatriated in this fashion. No subsequent group of prisoners was treated as leniently as were these marines; the document's remarks about torture proved to be portentous.

Little is known about the content of the indoctrination course at Kanggye except that it consisted of organized and compulsory lectures and discussion groups which were followed up with written examinations. In addition, the students had to 'prove' their sincerity and progress by appending their signatures to the so-called 'Stockholm Peace Appeal' which several of the Royal Marines signed in the hope of early release. This document was subsequently flourished under the noses of delegates to Communist-organized Peace Congress in the Swedish capital as proof of the Chinese good treatment of prisoners and their 'unanimous' desire for peace on Communist terms.

The Royal Marines imprisoned at Kanggye evidently hoped that by signing the petition they had a chance of early release. Politics was of less concern to them than their empty bellies, the bitter cold and the fact that four of their comrades had died from the want of elementary medical attention.

Following the political examinations, ostensibly to identify the most 'progressive' prisoners for early repatriation, the course ended on 2 March 1951. We do not know how the marines fared in their exams or whether Condron revealed any sign of promise to his captors. The evidence of his companions is contradictory, but after their repatriation two of his closest companions stated that what set him on the slippery slope to collaboration was that shortly before being captured he witnessed the cold-blooded execution of two Chinese p.o.w. by American marines. They implied that the incident affected him very deeply and that he must have been ruminating on it while at Kanggye. He was not chosen for release.

The manner in which the prisoners were selected for release was a timely warning to all the prisoners not to put any faith in Chinese promises. It was quite arbitrary and was made while all the marines were being taken from Kanggye towards the permanent camp at Pyoktong. The men who were not chosen were told that those who had been selected were being sent back to Kanggye to act as a reception committee for new arrivals. In fact, however, Kanggye was never again used and the selected men, including Marine R. Nicholls, were marched in the opposite direction, southwards to the battlefront to a spot opposite American lines. It is thought that the Chinese intended to put Nicholls across opposite a British sector after sending the Americans across to theirs. But on seeing the Americans depart, loaded with propaganda leaflets, Nicholls thought he had been tricked and made a desperate dash to join them. Before he had gone very far he was shot down by a volley from his guards and killed "while attempting to escape". Such was the compassion of Chinese 'Leniency'.

6

PEACE IN PYOKTONG

(Camp 5)

Almost from the outset of hostilities the U.N. Forces had sought in vain the whereabouts of the camps housing the hapless p.o.w. The ebb and flow of the war had allowed U.N. Intelligence to discover from North Korean p.o.w. in U.N. custody the wretched conditions in which about four thousand British and American prisoners were being held in tunnels and caves in their devastated land. After the Chinese entry into the war some information was forthcoming from the prisoners they repatriated through the front lines, but at this time the majority of the British p.o.w. were still in transit.

One of the reasons why the U.N. authorities were anxious to locate these camps was to avoid bombing them. Enquiries were made through the Red Cross in Switzerland, but they were refused admission into North Korea and were rebuffed by the Chinese on the grounds that they were 'an Imperialist spy organization'. Wide-ranging aerial reconnaissance also failed to locate the enemy's static prisoner of war camps, partly because the photo-interpreters were probably looking for characteristically 'Western' hutted camps surrounded by barbed wire fencing and watch-towers. When the Kaesong Peace talks began in July 1951 the Communist representatives claimed that they held 65,363 U.N. p.o.w, but they refused to give any indication of where they were being held. Later the Chinese produced a list of 11,000 they admitted to be holding, but were unable to say what had happened to the balance of 54,363. Instead, when pressed for information, they reluctantly drew circles round large areas of a map and hinted that the camps were within these areas. They were asked to mark the camps to prevent them from being bombed, but, as we shall see, they had very good reasons for not doing so and it was to be a long time before any of these PO. RO. markers, as they were called, were placed in prominent positions near some of the camps.

Their undue secrecy over such a humanitarian issue was far from comforting in view of the information available about the treatment being meted out by the North Koreans who had butchered a large number of their prisoners during their retreat to the north and had left a trail of bodies in their wake. The original figures produced by the Chinese included a large number of ROK prisoners, whom, it was later discovered, had been press-ganged into the North Korean army from hideous camps like the Kangdong Caves. It left about 8,000 British and American p.o.w. unaccounted for and our authorities were alarmed by reports coming in from diplomatic and other sources of gangs of ragged European-looking prisoners being seen in places as far apart as the Chinese port of Canton and the Manchurian port of Dairen. Fears began to grow about the possibility that many prisoners were being sent into slavery in Manchuria and Russia, as German p.o.w. had been during the Second World War. Although this was subsequently found to be mostly rumour, there was a grain of truth in it, for some prisoners, Canadian and American, were indeed held in Mukden and some of these did disappear into Russia.

Eventually U.N. attention was focused upon the mountains bordering the Yalu River and reconnaissance aircraft were sent to scour the area. Many never came back, having fallen victim to Russian Mig fighters, Chinese anti-aircraft guns and deception techniques used by the Chinese to lure aircraft into collision with mountain peaks. A Sabre aircraft, stripped of its armament and fitted with long-range fuel tanks and a powerful camera, succeeded in bringing back the first pictures of a typical Communist p.o.w. camp.

For almost a year a search had been made for conventional p.o.w. camps of the type used in Europe in the Second World War. Now it was discovered that the Communists' camps were ordinary Korean villages, deep in the mountains, partly occupied by Chinese troops and the native population. There was nothing to indicate that they were p.o.w. camps; there were no visible fences, no watchtowers or signs of guards, and, disturbingly, nothing to prevent the prisoners from escaping.

The first camp to be located was at Pyoktong, about a hundred miles inland from the west coast, a village on a peninsula that jutted into the Yalu River, giving many of the p.o.w. the impression that they were imprisoned on an island. Not far away was an important bridge over which the Chinese transported huge numbers of men and military supplies to Pyoktong, which they used as a frontier staging post on the way south to the battlefields, even after they had marked it as a p.o.w. camp with their PO. RO. markers. Before the Chinese overran the north, it had been one of the first places used by the North Koreans to accommodate

American prisoners during the winter of 1950, and because it had not been marked and was in frequent use for military traffic it had been bombed by U.N. aircraft and many of the prisoners had been killed.

The only other camp known to be holding British p.o.w. was near the town of Chongsong, sixty miles inland from the west coast, four miles south of the Yalu River and about thirty miles west of Pyoktong. The camp itself was some distance from the town and comprised hundreds of mud and wattle dwellings and a few larger buildings, notably old barrack huts said to have been erected by the Japanese army during the Second World War and now used to accommodate the camp staff. It had originally contained ROK army prisoners who had been moved elsewhere to house two thousand Americans. No PO. RO. markers were put down until after it had again been strafed by U.N. aircraft, killing some prisoners and wounding many others, including two British officers.

Both camps had originally been guarded by the North Koreans who were indifferent to the prisoners' welfare and had left them to their own devices and let them die of neglect. It was not until the camps were taken over by the Chinese in about April 1951 that some sort of order was restored by the imposition of the Lenient Policy which took no account of the terms of the Geneva Convention which entitles certain categories of prisoners such as the sick and wounded to special diets and accommodation, or of the segregation of prisoners according to rank. The Lenient Policy regarded all prisoners as equal, ignoring rank, health and other humane considerations.

In both camps the prisoners were divided into groups of twelve or sixteen, regardless of rank, and each group was herded into a room about ten feet square. In this way about sixty or seventy prisoners were crowded into each Korean house. At first there were no beds, no blankets, no fuel and no means of keeping out the icy draughts from the lousy dilapidated hovels and only later were some prisoners issued with three old army greatcoats per room. Eventually the Chinese did issue all prisoners with quilted overcoats and one thin blanket.

The primitive accommodation dictated the way the prisoners were organized. Each roomful of men became a squad and each household a platoon. Clusters of nearby houses in various parts of the village became a 'compound' and the occupants formed a company. Within a given company area the houses occupied by the prisoners were interspersed by others occupied either by the Chinese staff or by villagers. The company 'compounds' were likewise separated by tracks, roads, barns and buildings occupied by the camp staff or by villagers. This primitive arrangement very effectively prevented prisoners in any one platoon from mixing freely or communicating with all the other platoons in the same company, without being seen by the staff. It also prevented the prisoners from one company wandering into another company 'compound'. Occupying a dominant position in the centre of each village was the Chinese P.O.W. Corps headquarters, the nerve centre of the camp, with adjacent make-shift jails and interrogation rooms. On the fringes of the villages were outlying shacks, bunkers, caves and holes in the ground which were used for segregation, torture and punishment purposes.

Each company was supervised by at least two Chinese company officers, one for administration and one for discipline, supported by three assistants, a political 'instructor', a messing officer, an interpreter and a large number of soldiers. In addition, under the company staff were platoon and assistant platoon officers, interpreters and supernumeraries. Each platoon was therefore supervised by at least one Chinese officer and some had two or three to maintain order. Altogether there were almost as many Chinese in the camps as there were prisoners, but relatively few of them were scattered about the compounds as sentries or wandering patrols. Most were employed in top-heavy administrative duties.

In both Pyoktong and Chongsong there were areas of open ground which were used for assembly areas for all the prisoners in the camp for harangues, political lectures and speeches, and only on these occasions were the prisoners able to mix with or communicate with prisoners from other platoons, companies and compounds.

The administrative advantages of the whole system are fairly obvious. No special provision had to be made for accommodation, food, health, comfort or messing arrangements according to rank, as required under the terms of the Geneva Convention. The Lenient Policy spread its misery equally among all. Despite the lessons learned during the Kanggye experiment, the political officers still regarded their British and American prisoners as uneducated, and especially as politically uneducated peasants. They also regarded them as intellectually and racially inferior. At the beginning the Chinese clearly expected compliance and ready acceptance of their organization and leadership and had no conception of the scale and nature of the opposition that they would encounter.

The history of Camp 5 at Pyoktong falls conveniently into three phases. The first was a period during which the inmates struggled to survive under the North Korean administration, whose policy was to allow them to rot, while at the same time allowing a handful of Chinese officers to carry out a desultory programme of indoctrination and interrogation. The second period began in April 1951 when the Chinese assumed control and put their Lenient Policy into effect. It was a period of intensive reorganization and politicization of treatment, culminating in the purge of the 'reactionary' elements. The third phase followed the transfer of the 'reactionaries' to special punishment camps, thus allowing the political consolidation of the activities of the remainder. It saw the steady growth of political activities among these p.o.w., finally outrivalling the activities of the Pyongyang Peace Fighters in their production of political propaganda and produced the highest percentage of 'progressives' of any of the Chinese-controlled camps in Korea.

The first phase began with the arrival of the survivors of the January column of British prisoners on 6 March 1951. They were all suffering from malnutrition and diseases, especially respiratory diseases and were worn out by eight weeks of marching in bitter winter weather. Their morale was very low. But for the courageous and unsparing efforts of their senior officer, Major M.D. Ryan, and a handful of officers and optimists, many more of them would have died of despair. Already the military chain of command of the column and standards of conduct had broken down. The enemy had kept a watchful eye on the conduct of the British officers and had partially succeeded in preventing them from influencing their men by placing them at the head of the column. In the column itself the instructions of the escorts were passed down to the prisoners through the squad leaders, appointed by the enemy regardless of rank. Few of the prisoners now paid any attention to their NCOs, whom the Chinese had deprived of their authority. Although this might seem a poor reflection on their abilities to command their subordinates, it complies with the terms of the Geneva Convention which vests authority for Other Ranks in their elected representatives, irrespective of rank. And the Chinese had, to some extent, allowed the rankers to pick their squad leaders. The hardships of the march had seriously weakened the social cohesion of nearly all groups. They were perilously close to death and in these circumstances it is not surprising that self-interest and self-preservation counted for more than the stripes on the arm, or, for that matter, upon the tenuous authority the Chinese had vested in their appointed squad leaders. The men were apt to follow anybody whose abilities brought them a measure of stability to their chaotic existence and some food or better shelter.

By the time the prisoners reached Pyoktong about a third had already decided that it was more prudent to keep their heads down and cooperate with their captors, at least until they found ways of avoiding doing so. Few of them could have foreseen what their decisions would entail and they all fervently hoped that conditions on arrival would not be worse, that the Chinese would honour their promises, repeated throughout the march, that they would be well looked after when they reached their destination.

It is not difficult to imagine their feelings when they finally limped into a derelict village on the Pyoktong peninsula. It reeked of death and disease and was inhabited by several hundred American scarecrows who were dying at the rate of twenty a day, rising to a death toll of over one thousand.

The new arrivals quickly discovered that their Chinese escorts had little say in the running of the camp, which was under the control of the North Koreans. The morale of the American inmates had long since plunged to its lowest level and their behaviour had likewise disintegrated to the meanest, lowest levels of self-interest. According to post-war American official reports, the compounds were being run by racketeers and thieves. There were frequent instances of dying prisoners being thrown out of their huts to let the icy winds finish them off to save their companions the trouble of looking after them and allow their rations to be drawn by the survivors until their deaths were discovered by the camp authorities. It was common to ignore the pleas of the sick for such elementary necessities as a drink of water. The black market operated on a grand scale. A few prisoners would appropriate the rations of a whole company and trade it with the North Koreans or sell it to other prisoners at exorbitant prices in dollars or in the universal currency of tobacco.

This deplorable state of affairs made a deep impression on the new arrivals, a high percentage of whom immediately became virulently anti-American without the intervention of the Chinese propagandists. A more charitable minority of the British prisoners blamed it on the American way of life for fostering competitiveness, even in adversity.

The indifference of the camp authorities in allowing these things to happen indicated to many of the British prisoners that there were opportunities for maintaining law and order by means which the Chinese had forbidden, that it was possible for the actual and natural leaders to assert their authority, at least among the British prisoners. In any case the prevailing situation made the British p.o.w. realize that their own survival would depend upon them sticking together, upon maintaining elementary values and codes of conduct as well as their social cohesion. These lessons were driven home to them at a time when there was a tendency to relax after the hardships of the march. They retained some of their traditional characteristics, especially their compassion for their sicker companions and the knack of collectively fending for themselves under adverse conditions in the face of two larger pressure groups, the Americans and the Chinese. The awful example of the Americans forced the British prisoners into closer social cohesion at a critical time.

From the outset the British officers were accommodated in a compound well away from their men. Nevertheless, the ORs used their own initiatives. By guile and stealth they began raiding nearby unoccupied dwellings for materials with which to repair their own dilapidated hovels. Those caught were savagely beaten up by the North Koreans "for damaging the people's property". But the cannibalization of the unoccupied huts continued on a grand scale for several days until the camp authorities relented and gave permission for the British prisoners to repair their quarters.

Despite these and other spontaneous measures to ease their lot, life for the British p.o.w. during the first month in Pyoktong was as precarious as it had been on the march. Food was grossly inadequate and diseases were rampant. Captain A.M. Ferrie, the medical officer of the Royal Ulster Rifles, was at first permitted to do what he could. He was allowed to visit the OR's compounds at regular intervals, but he could do little more than instruct the men on elementary hygiene. The lousy, overcrowded quarters resulted in epidemics of dysentery which were impossible to curb. When, eventually, the Chinese took control of the camp, he and an American doctor made repeated representations for more drugs and dressings and supplies were slightly increased on the strict understanding that they must be shared equally among all the prisoners. When the doctors pointed out that the meagre supplies should be conserved and used upon the less hopeless cases, they were loudly rebuked and told that their suggestion was 'undemocratic'. Ferrie reckoned that, had his proposal been permitted, fifty per cent of those who died could have been saved. The result of being 'democratic' was that every single prisoner who fell seriously ill at this time subsequently died. The Chinese insisted on the very sick being fed on a diet of seaweed soup. Those who could swallow this stinking brew died during spasms of vomiting; those who could not face it died of starvation and their diseases.

Throughout March 1951 batches of prisoners continued to arrive, including the Royal Marines from Kanggye. Among the latter was Marine Condron, who, according to his two closest friends, already viewed the behaviour of the Americans with acute disgust. His views were reinforced by what he found at Pyoktong, and neither he nor his two companions expressed any compassion when they saw sick and bedraggled Americans being savagely beaten by the North Koreans. Neither did they express any sympathy for those of their fellow countrymen who were consigned to the 'holes' for petty infractions, or for those who were dying in considerable numbers for the want of adequate food, medical attention and shelter. They quickly came to believe that the Chinese in the camp were doing everything they could in difficult circumstances aggravated by the American bombing of supply lines.

This attitude was shared by many others. Although there were few Chinese in the camp, their behaviour contrasted markedly with that of the North Koreans. They seemed genuinely anxious to alleviate the plight of the prisoners, few of whom suspected that their concern stemmed primarily from their embarrassment at the damage the savage behaviour of North Koreans was causing to their Lenient Policy and their own repeated promises of leniency.

One group of British prisoners had cause to be especially grateful to the Chinese. This was a party of wounded who, soon after capture, had been transported to Pyongyang by train to a Chinese hospital where they received timely and adequate treatment. They counted themselves lucky, as indeed they were, since the majority of their stricken companions had been left to die on the battlefield or in filthy transit camps. Significantly many of this lucky group early began collaborating with the Chinese.

Soon after reaching Pyoktong the prisoners were allocated to their quarters, up to fifteen men to a room of a Korean house. Each roomful of men constituted a squad and one of their number was told to act as the squad leader. Most of the British prisoners were put to work cutting and hauling timber from the hillsides to heat the quarters of their Korean guards, although they themselves were denied any means of heating their own dilapidated quarters. Periodically they were assembled on open ground to listen to two Chinese political officers with only a very super-ficial knowledge of their subjects delivering compulsory lectures in execrable English. They commanded attention only because afterwards the lectures were followed by supervision. Each squad had been compelled to appoint a 'monitor' whose duty it was to report to the camp political officers to collect questions for group discussion. These had to be taken back to the huts where squad members were supposed to talk them over and prepare suitable answers, expressing, of course, a Communist point of view. Any attempt to return a 'capitalist' answer resulted in a visit from a Chinese political officer who, ignoring time and meals, would argue with the culprits until fatigue and empty bellies compelled them to agree that the Communist answer was 'correct'. The pathetic part of all this was that few of the ORs were capable of refuting the enemy's arguments. They were woefully ignorant of the history of their own country and those who were not were disinclined to refute the half-truths and fallacies of logic. With the British officers it was a very different story.

The Chinese had early detailed the SBO, Major Ryan, to act as squad monitor and he had refused to accept for discussion any question that was based upon fallacious assumptions. As nearly all of them were of this kind a successful blockade was established. Moreover all the British officers had an exasperating habit of jumping to their feet during the mass assemblies for lectures and discussions to challenge the speakers on points of fact, logic and opinion. They had to be gagged by repeated warnings about their 'hostile attitudes' and the penalties for those who put themselves outside the benefits of the Lenient Policy. To prevent a 'conspiracy' they were re-squadded, one each to different American squads.

By the end of the first phase of captivity most of the prisoners realized that their survival depended upon co-operation during lectures and discussions. Failure to do so brought collective punishment to the members of the squad in the form of additional lectures, tutorials, supervision and missed meals. For men on the verge of starvation the latter was a serious matter, an unacceptable penalty to pay for refusing to listen to political claptrap.

On 1 April 1951 the Chinese assumed complete control of the camp and the North Koreans departed. Pyoktong became Camp No. 5. All the inmates were assembled to listen to an introductory speech by a senior Chinese officer. It lasted for four and a half hours and began in terms as follows (recorded verbatim in shorthand by an unknown British p.o.w. and smuggled out when he was repatriated):–

Everyone in the aggressive force is guilty of crime and no leniency is required. The United States aggression is a good reason for exacting a blood debt. But surrendered soldiers are, nevertheless, treated humanely by the Chinese People's Volunteers who will not exact their blood debt, as is their right, providing you show yourselves willing to learn the truth. Those of you who refuse to co-operate will be regarded as war criminals, not entitled to the benefits of our Lenient Policy. To help you learn the truth a new daily programme has been arranged. Henceforth you will be allowed to study for eight hours every day. The new routine is as follows:
  0600   Study
  0800   Breakfast

0830	Study
1200	Lunch
1400	Group discussion and time to write answers to set questions
1600	Supper

The rest of the day will be free.

Throughout this long address, the speaker continually reminded his audience that because they had participated in a war of aggression against the peace-loving peoples of North Korea they were war criminals and as such could rightfully be executed. He insisted that South Korea had started the war, that the Americans had intervened unlawfully, that the prisoners should be eternally grateful for being spared their lives and allowed the opportunity to learn the truth. Under the circumstances only criminals would be ungrateful and, by implication, would be treated as criminals if they were unappreciative of the chances they were being given.

Many other new arrangements were announced. The domestic routine and management of prisoners' affairs was to be reorganized. The squad leaders were to be given new responsibilities. They were brought together and were handed printed instructions about the nature of their duties. The following is an extract:–

Squad Leaders are responsible for:–
a) Ensuring that all prisoners strictly observe the regulations.
b) Reporting all happenings in their squads.
c) Carrying out bed checks morning and evening.
d) Reporting the opinions of squad members concerning political studies and camp routine.

In other words the squad leaders were required to be overt informers. Snap checks on their capabilities soon revealed the identities of those who were being dilatory in the execution of their duties and they were removed and replaced with others more 'progressive' in their attitudes.

It was also announced that each company of prisoners would elect six sub-committees to run Messing, Sanitation, Mail, Entertainments, Sports and Library and Information services. These sub-committees would constitute the company Daily Life Committees whose members would be eligible for election to the Camp Daily Life Committee, which would be responsible for co-ordinating all the various activities and negotiating with the camp authorities.

63

It all sounded very promising after the chaos of the North Korean regime under which there had been no mail, no sports, no entertainment and no library. Sanitary and cookhouse fatigues had been avoided if at all possible. Now, apparently, everything was going to be well-organized and the prisoners were at last being granted some of their rights under the terms of the Geneva Convention. It was some time before the p.o.w. discovered that they were being cheated on all counts.

For several days after the introduction of the new regime the prisoners cautiously submitted to the reorganization and the daily dose of indoctrination and political studies, watching for weaknesses that could be exploited to advantage. Soon unoccupied dwellings were mysteriously demolished and it was some time before the Chinese discovered that they were being used for firewood to provide their captives with fires, previously denied to them no matter what the weather. A few culprits and scapegoats were dragged off for interrogation and consigned to the 'holes' (narrow trenches in the ground) until they agreed to confess publicly to "destroying the people's property".

One morning a British sergeant, C.J. Taylor, refused to salute his captors during the morning roll-call and was marched away for interrogation while the rest of the assembled prisoners were made to stand and shiver for fifteen minutes in the icy cold.

By 9 April, barracking and booing during lectures and discussions had become fairly commonplace and ribald catcalls greeted the Chinese speakers from unseen voices amidst the large assemblies. It was exceedingly difficult for the Chinese to identify the culprits, though they attempted to do so by posting lookouts at suitable points. Many prisoners slept through the assemblies, having already found the means of getting round the subsequent discussion periods. It was all very easy. The more influential members of the squads leaned on the squad leaders and monitors to encourage them to be lax in the execution of their unsavoury duties. A volunteer would undertake to listen to the lectures and prepare written answers afterwards on behalf of the whole squad. The rest would sleep or play cards. The Chinese endeavoured to combat this ruse by sending their platoon officers into the compounds to make snap checks, but there were not enough of them to visit all huts and all rooms in the huts simultaneously and the prisoners soon devised a system of warning of their approach.

Eventually the Chinese identified the resisters by a well-tried and characteristically Maoist trick of "letting a hundred flowers bloom". During lectures the prisoners were encouraged to voice their honest opinions on the running of the camp and the content and methods of their political education. The prisoners were embarrassingly frank, thus allowing the Chinese look-outs to identify the speakers. After a time these prisoners were re-mustered to form 'reactionary' squads and, as their numbers grew, into 'reactionary' platoons accommodated in separate huts to prevent them spreading their 'reactionary' infection. They were subjected to extra lessons, individual supervision and continuous surveillance. A trusted informer, a British prisoner, was injected into the midst of each group to report on their behaviour.

Although most of the British prisoners found the indoctrination tiresome, and most of it unintelligible, there were some who took a lively interest in the proceedings. There were a few, especially among the reservists, who had an active and long-standing interests in politics, including a few members of Trade Unions. A few were Communist Party members or sympathizers and others belonged to socialist or left-wing parties or organizations. None of them had ever received any formal training in politics and welcomed the present opportunities to improve their knowledge. There were quite a few who, out of sheer boredom, listened intently to fill an intellectual vacuum and developed an interest in political philosophy, of a sort, for the first time in their lives. All these men were readily identifiable by friend and foe alike. They were too conscientious and sincere during lectures and discussions. Many visited the camp headquarters for material to read and were given old copies of the *Shanghai News* or *The Daily Worker*. Others asked for books because it was easier to read books than to listen to the fractured English of the Chinese indoctrinators and the agonizing speeches of the political officers. Some went even further and asked for extra tuition from the experts who gleefully rubbed their hands and offered flattering encouragement. But there was a price to be paid. They were soon compelled to 'prove' their sincerity by carrying out unsavoury little tasks such as informing on their colleagues. The Chinese were preparing to introduce a little 'democracy' into the domestic affairs of the camp.

After receiving the order to set up the Daily Life committees the prisoners were permitted to nominate and freely elect their company representatives. But the Chinese let it be known that they would be ratifying all appointments. Within a month the freely elected representatives were being quietly turned out of office for 'inefficiency', for putting themselves outside the benefits of the Lenient Policy or for taking liberties that revealed their 'hostile attitudes' or on feeble excuses such as 'changed situations'. Several of the more dominant members were arrested and flung into the 'holes'. It soon became clear that the Chinese would only ratify the appointments of those whom they favoured for political or internal security reasons and were clearing the way for these to rise to the top. The same veto was applied to the squad leaders and monitors. Many of the old ones were deprived of their offices and were replaced almost exclusively by the 'conscientious' students. Eventually it became clear that the domestic life of the camp and the entire organization had fallen into the hands of a half a dozen or so leading 'progressives', (ultimately known to all prisoners as The Big Wheel) and that the 'free' elections had been a sham.

The Camp Daily Life Committee was presided over by a Chinese officer whose deputy was Marine Andrew Condron, a leading 'progressive'. After a suitable period of training Condron was promoted to the chair by 'a popular vote of the Committee' and presided over the whole organization, the chief political stooge in the camp. Some of the prisoners stated that he was both popular and able and had the confidence of many British and American prisoners. Some said he did a good job and achieved much for their benefit, by which they meant benefit to the 'progressives'. There was some evidence to suggest that he came to exert an uncanny influence over several of the Chinese personnel due to his by no means trivial knowledge of Communist standard works to interpret for them difficult political concepts.

Whether or not he was genuinely elected into high office by the prisoners or owed his position to Chinese interference will never be known for certain but the chances are that the elections were rigged by methods presently to be described.

To the outside world the creation of the camp Daily Life Committee, which was trumpeted in the Communist press and propaganda, added strength to their claim to be treating the prisoners humanely and in accordance with the Geneva Convention. Little did the world suspect that the function of the Committee and the sub-committees was primarily to produce political propaganda and compel the prisoners to live in a totalitarian social system. They were inextricably linked to the squad leader and monitor system, spying on the behaviour of all prisoners at every level in order to identify and quell any rebellious behaviour and prevent it from upsetting the supposed political unity of the entire camp in its condemnation of American aggression and its demands for peace on Communist terms. Within nine months of its creation the camp Daily Life Committee and its sub-committees were churning out propaganda and issuing bulletins and statements on behalf of *all* the prisoners in the camp.

But there was one group of prisoners that was never allowed to be represented; that was the British and American officers who had been segregated into a separate compound after their influence had been recognized by their captors. The Chinese refused to ratify all but one of their freely elected candidates and they in turn refused to elect the Chinese-nominated candidates to the various Daily Life Committees. The exception was Major Ryan, the SBO, who was the Messing Officer. The Chinese allowed his name to go forward, probably in the hope that they would be able to exploit his popularity, and if not that, allow him enough rope to exhibit his patently 'hostile attitude' and provide an excuse for dismissing him and replacing him with their own nominee. In the meantime the freely elected representatives ran the compound's domestic affairs and refused to become a propaganda organ. Clearly the Chinese were not going to accept this defeat, which not only made them lose face but also set a bad example to the OR's compounds. The officers recognized that there would be an inevitable showdown, but few foresaw its savagery.

Among the Chinese staff dealing with the officers' compound were two who were to gain notoriety, although at present they held relatively minor posts. The first of this pair was Ding Fang, who was to become the Commandant of a camp set up exclusively for officer prisoners. He was about thirty-eight years of age, of medium height, had a pallid skin and fine bones and narrow eyes that glistened like a snake's. He spoke no English. The other officer was Wong, destined to become the chief interpreter to the officers' camp, Ding Fang's right-hand man, christened DP or Dirty Picture Wong by the prisoners due to his crude remarks about their collection of pin-up girls which he delighted in confiscating for himself. He was a massive man, even by Western standards, and spoke fair English with an American accent which he had acquired as a former student of Shanghai University. He had a bad reputation for abusing American p.o.w. in a camp known as the Valley Camp where he had been an interrogator.

Their first brush with the officer-prisoners occurred during a discussion period when one of the American officers, Major T.A. Hume, indiscreetly remarked that the question under discussion was not worth the paper it was written on. He was immediately arrested and charged with "publicly insulting the workers of the Chinese paper-making industry". Without trial, he was flung into prison and for three weeks was badly beaten and tortured into making a confession. He was then returned to the officers' compound to spy on his fellow prisoners and was threatened with further punishment if he failed in this mission. His savage treatment had left him with several injuries and had seriously weakened his general health. He told his brother officers that he had been released to spy on them and begged them not to say anything incriminating in his presence as he felt he could not stand any more beating. He confided to his friends that he no longer wished to live and despite their efforts to raise his morale he died two weeks after his release from jail.

The second clash between the prisoners and Ding Fang and his thugs occurred when four American officers were recaptured after an escape attempt. There had been many attempts in the past and upon recapture the culprits had been punished. This time, however, the culprits were to be used to force terms on the recalcitrant, freely elected members of the Daily Life Committee, which included the Senior U.N. Officer, known as SUNO. Incidentally, the American forces, unlike the British forces, had no common system for nominating the senior officer where all three Services were represented, because of inter-service rivalry. Their three services regarded themselves equal; none had recognized precedence over the others. In the British services the Navy is the senior service and the RAF the junior. Where the senior officer of one service is of equal rank to those of the others, the SBO would be the Naval officer; if the senior officers were an Army officer of equal rank to the senior Air Force officer, the SBO would be the Army officer. Where the senior officer of one service clearly outranks the others, whether Navy, Army or Air Force, that officer becomes the SBO. The lack of a jointly accepted system among American officers caused much wrangling in the Korean p.o.w. camps until circumstances compelled them to work together for their own good. So they devised a system based upon time-in-rank.

In Pyoktong the officer the Americans appointed was an army Captain who was also the SUNO. He was to be held responsible for the escapes. He and the four escapers were arrested and beaten with clubs and fists until they agreed to confess to their 'crimes'. The SUNO refused to do so and was flogged again and given twenty-four hours to reconsider his position. When he again refused his hands were tied behind his back and he was marched across the compound in full view of the other prisoners to a scaffold where he was hanged by his wrists behind his back until he agreed to confess some ten hours later. He was cut down and, prompted by his torturers, dictated a humiliating confession which was handed to his brother officers who were ordered to pass a suitable sentence for his 'crimes'. While they pondered upon what they should do in this situation the victim was further ill-treated to hasten their decision. They eventually agreed to sentence him to thirty days' solitary confinement, the maximum permitted under the Geneva Convention for escaping, in the belief that if they showed any leniency the Chinese would impose a much harsher sentence. The Chinese accepted the decision and the SUNO was immediately released on condition that he spied on his fellow officers. He had taken a terrible beating and his hands were partly paralysed. He agreed to the terms of his release and became a pawn of his captors.

The escapers were similarly ill-treated and all five, upon their release, were sent into the officers' compound to collect signatures for a 'Petition for the Cessation of Hostilities'. The couriers themselves were examples of what could happen to anybody who refused to sign. All the officers signed, but because there were too many Joe Soaps, John Does, Davy Crocketts, John Smiths, John Bulls, Mickey Mouses and Fanny Snowwhites among the signatories and so many other signatures had been grossly distorted by signing with left hands, the document was never given any publicity.

These two examples of the Chinese brutality heralded a major 'Peace' offensive in which all the Pyoktong prisoners were compelled to play a major role. Already the Pyongyang Peace Fighters were churning out masses of propaganda on behalf of the North Koreans. Now the Chinese began their own campaign. It started in June 1951 with an order to the prisoners to form 'Peace Committees'. All squads, including those in the officers' compound, were told to elect representatives who would then go forward as candidates for platoon and company elections. The elected representatives would then go forward for election to a camp Peace Committee from whom a member would be elected as a representative of an inter-camp Central Peace Committee. All elections were to be 'democratic', that is to say would have to be ratified by the camp authorities. Failure to vote and spoiling ballot papers would be regarded as serious 'hostile' acts.

In each of the ORs' compounds the prisoners were assembled to cast their votes under the watchful eyes of the Chinese who looked at every piece of paper to see that it had not been spoiled and a Chinese officer and several members of the Daily Life Committee stood by each unsealed ballot box "to ensure fair play". Voting took place on a single list of approved candidates, all of them 'progressives'.

Once the company Peace Committees had been elected they were ordered to convene a general meeting for the purpose of electing the Camp 5 Central Peace Committee. Only the elected members of the company committees were eligible for nomination. A mass meeting was called of all the ORs to hear the election speeches of the nominees, each of whom in turn mounted a rostrum to give a résumé of his life and his reasons for seeking office. The proceedings were lavishly photographed by the propagandists. After they had all had their say, the assembly cast their votes as before, under surveillance.

The Chinese did not keep faith even with their closely supervised 'democratic' election, at least in so far as the elections of the President and Vice President of the Central Committee were concerned. The election results bore little relation to the outcome; the prisoners were merely going through the motions. There were two important witnesses to these elections. One was Major Ryan, whose presence will shortly be explained; the other was the man 'elected' as Vice President, a British Private and one of the leading progressives, who was interrogated by the author at length after his early repatriation during Operation Little Switch, the exchange of sick and wounded in April 1953. From these two sources it was clear that before the elections took place the Chinese had pre-determined the outcome. Their chosen candidate for the job of President was the American SUNO, so recently 'broken' by interrogation, but to get him elected it was first necessary to get him elected to the company committee in the officers' compound, which proved to be difficult since the officers stubbornly refused to nominate him and insisted upon holding a genuinely free election of their own nominees. The Chinese equally stubbornly refused to ratify the prisoners' chosen candidates and finally cancelled the elections on the grounds that they were 'undemocratic'. Nevertheless, they detailed several officers, including Major Ryan, to attend the mass meeting of all the rest of the prisoners in the camp to lend substance to their pretence that the officers were as enthusiastic about forming the Peace Committees as their men. But the officers were not allowed to vote or take any active part in the proceedings. Ryan and his fellow officers were compelled to witness the OR candidates making fools of themselves on the rostrum, knowing full well that the outcome had already been decided.

The Vice President discovered from his own enquiries after his 'unanimous' election that several of his 'progressive' colleagues had received more votes than he had, which was scarcely very surprising since he had not attended the meeting because of a bout of influenza and therefore had not made a speech from the rostrum along with the other candidates.

It is uncertain how many of the British prisoners put themselves forward for these elections, but there were many progressives more suitable for the job of Vice President than the man elected, if it was intended that he should make a generous contribution to a peace campaign. The

70

man chosen was an insipid, timid character who must have known that his appointment would attract much publicity and would land him in trouble with the Chinese if he did not do their bidding and with the British authorities if he did. Condron was an obvious front-runner, but in choosing the man that they did one senses some political chicanery on the part of the Chinese. They wanted an ineffective stooge to palm off on to the North Koreans for their rival outfit in Pyongyang. He was sent as the Camp 5 representative to join the Peace Fighters and found the North Koreans' hospitality infinitely less agreeable than the Chinese. He spent the next six months living in misery and squalor until he and all the other Peace Fighters were transferred to Pyoktong to face a much-changed situation.

The formation of the Central Peace Committee prepared the way for a major Chinese propaganda offensive timed to coincide with the opening of the Kaesong Peace Talks in July. By then the Peace organization possessed tentacles that reached down into every one of the ORs' squads through the camp and company, platoon and squad peace representatives and committees which were in the hands of the same men who comprised the Daily Life committees, whose functions were almost entirely political. Altogether about twenty per cent of the British ORs in Pyoktong were by now actively collaborating with the enemy and were being used to influence the politically uncommitted prisoners, the majority of whom had so far balanced themselves on the razor's edge, undecided on which side it was most prudent to fall. They were about to be prodded into accepting life under Communism.

The first by no means gentle prod came from the squad monitors. From the humble beginnings as messenger boys to the Chinese platoon political officers, their functions gradually changed to stool pigeons and agitators. Those who failed to reach an adequate degree of collaboration had long since been removed from office and many were now languishing in cells or in the 'holes'. Their replacements were required to make regular reports on the political 'attitudes' and 'progress' of each member of their squads, basing their judgements on the way they were developing during discussion periods and remarks passed in unguarded moments. These were reported daily to the Chinese political and security officers respectively responsible for running the political education and informer networks. Upon repatriation the squad monitors hotly denied that their role was akin to pernicious informing, claiming that their role had been entirely political. Yet they must have known the consequences of their reports. Adverse reports resulted in extra political instruction for the culprits, the more stubborn of whom were beaten up or sent to prison for their 'hostile attitudes' after being re-squaded into 'reactionary' platoons. The squad leaders and monitors were the instruments by which the Chinese brought about the destruction of inter-personal trust and the social cohesion of the sub-groups comprising each squad and their replacement by a Communist structure and system of group and individual control.

In August 1951, four months after the Chinese had taken control of the camp, two British sergeants, twelve ORs and a larger number of Americans, all so-called reactionaries, were curtly ordered to pack their belongings. The British element included Sergeant C.J. Taylor, already punished for refusing to salute the Chinese, Rifleman J.T. Kelly and Rifleman J.R. Bartlett, all three of whom had been forced to dig bunkers and clear the battlefield soon after they were captured. Also included was Marine P.D. Murphy, the natural leader of the marines at Koto-ri and Kanggye, Riflemen J.T. Alexander and J. Shaw, two particularly obstinate students of a reactionary platoon. They had been planning to escape with Sergeant Taylor and Rifleman J.J. Buckley who acquired fame for possessing a particularly dangerous item of contraband, a camera. Just how Buckley had managed to conceal a camera from numerous searches remains a mystery, but it was a major feat of ingenuity. His feat came to grief, like so many others, as a direct result of informing; he was arrested and accused of being a secret agent and ordered to confess. When he refused he was savagely beaten about the head with clubs and fists and sent to prison for two months. As a direct result of his mistreatment he lost the power of speech and remained incoherent for the rest of his two years in captivity. After his release from prison he returned to his compound and thrashed the British soldier he believed had betrayed him.

This party of incorrigible reactionaries was transferred in lorries to a new camp, Camp 3 branch 1, at Changsong, thirty miles downriver from Pyoktong and so became the first Anglo-American group to be segregated in a special camp for unco-operative prisoners. Here there was a harsher regime; there was no political study, no mail and a much lower standard of living. They remained there for the better part of a year, after which they were dispersed into various other camps for 'reactionaries', one of which was the penal camp at Song-Ni, notorious for its liberal use of the 'holes'.

With the removal of the more overt reactionaries, the work of the in-doctrinators proceeded with much less opposition and interruption, aided and abetted by a growing body of progressives to keep the remainder neutralized and pliant for the rest of the war.

In September 1951 Colonel Carne, the most senior British officer in captivity, was posted into the camp in an attempt to break his influence with the officers in Camp 1 at Chongsong. But his presence had a sobering effect on all ranks and stiffened the behaviour of both the British and American prisoners, particularly those in the officers' compound. On 2 October all the officers in Camp 5 were transferred to a new camp exclusively for officers at Pin Chon-Ni, to which the fanatical Ding Fang was posted as Commandant.

The departure of the officers still left the senior NCOs in the camp. It is not known if these were confined in a compound of their own or whether they were mixed with the ORs and junior NCOs. Like the officers, they had been warned repeatedly that they would be punished if they asserted their authority and they must have been leading some sort of resistance because they were all moved out into a camp of their own at Kuuptong in August 1952.

Soon after the removal of the officers the Chinese mounted a propaganda offensive in the camp, requiring the prisoners to write protests, peace appeals, petitions to influential bodies and people in the West and to send greetings to Communist 'front' organizations all over the world. The peak was reached in November and December 1951 with a flood of written propaganda and broadcasts over Peking radio, all supposedly produced spontaneously by the prisoners themselves. The majority of this material had been produced at the instigation of the Chinese by the leading progressives who formed the Central Peace and Daily Life Committees within the camp and who were living in a special compound where they were being rewarded with privileges for their co-operation. It was into this compound that occidental visitors were taken to meet the 'happy' prisoners, visitors like two correspondents of Communist newspapers, Wilfred Burchett and Alan Winnington, and Monica Felton, Michael Shapiro and Jack Gasker. Felton was the chairman of the British National Assembly for Women, a Communist 'front' organization, and Shapiro and Gaster were Communist Party members. They were fed with glowing accounts of the Chinese 'leniency' and were impressed by the amount of 'freedom' the progressives enjoyed. They subsequently produced impressive reports for press and radio saying how well the British p.o.w. were being treated and said nothing about the awful conditions they had seen in the North Korean-controlled camps that they had visited earlier in the year.

At this time less than thirty per cent of the British prisoners in Camp 5 were actively collaborating with the enemy; the remainder were signing petitions under protest and threats of cuts in their rations and deterioration of their living conditions if they failed to sign.

In December, after the propaganda offensive, compulsory political studies suddenly ceased, having apparently outlived their purpose. They were replaced with voluntary study, supposedly at the request of the prisoners themselves. The first two voluntary study groups were in mathematics and literature, Communist literature, needless to say. The latter was reputed to have split into two groups as a result of moves made by Condron and six other progressives who broke away from literary studies to found a group studying political theory. This latter group boasted a rapid growth in membership until it ultimately possessed fifty regular attenders among the British p.o.w., including the former Peace Fighters of Pyongyang, and many casual attenders. In due course the notebooks of some of these prisoners fell into the author's hands and he can testify to the thoroughness of the political education they received in Communism.

By March 1952 fifty eight per cent of the British p.o.w. in Pyoktong had co-operated with the enemy in political activities, a figure that remained unchanged for the rest of the war. A year later, when the officers and sergeants had been removed to camps of their own and the active reactionaries had been condemned to punishment camps, ninety-two percent of the British ORs in Camp 5 had participated in Communist propaganda activities to a greater or lesser degree.

The success which the Chinese apparently achieved with their propaganda activities in Camp 5 was due in no small part to a small and active clique of progressives. They proved invaluable to the Chinese by helping them to modify their original Lenient Policy and amend it to a p.o.w. population that was far better educated than the illiterate Chinese peasant soldiers for which it had been originally designed. The original political lectures had been pitched at entirely the wrong level and were based upon ludicrous Dickensian concepts of the British way of life. Without the information supplied by the progressive prisoners about the real social situation in Britain, the Chinese would have continued to discredit their own arguments with their ludicrous misconceptions of Western lifestyles, inviting immediate rejection of their arguments as well as jeers and catcalls at their comic ideas. However, even when their propaganda had been modified, without the suppression of the authority of NCOs and the removal of all those capable of countering the fallacious arguments and the outright propaganda, as well as all those who were simply resentful at their imprisonment and mistreatment, the Chinese could not have succeeded in the political exploitation of the remainder. The progressives would have been counterbalanced in numbers by the officers, NCOs and reactionary ORs. Only by dismantling the prisoners' military command and control structure and destroying the mores and thus the cohesion of the traditional social groupings by identifying and exploiting the weak, and the use of progressives to pinpoint the reactionary elements for removal, could the remaining prisoners be forced to acquiesce under a Communist regime.

Never before in recent history had an enemy taken such a close personal interest in the attitudes and behaviour of every single prisoner, however humble.

7

SPRING EVACUATION

The Imjin River battle started late on the night of 25 April 1951 and lasted until the Glosters' positions were overrun by the sheer weight of numbers of Chinese, despite the enemy's appalling casualties. The exhausted British troops were scattered over a wide area after they had been compelled to surrender and the majority found themselves in a state of profound shock.

Their Commanding Officer was Lieut. Colonel J.P. Carne who was soon to discover that he was the most senior British Officer to be captured by the Chinese. His deputy was Major Denis Harding. The Support Company Commander was Major 'Sam' Weller who was to become one of the most influential officers in captivity. The Adjutant to the Battalion, the young Captain Anthony Farrar-Hockley, was soon to disappear on the first of his numerous escape attempts and was to become noted for making more attempts than any other prisoner, British or American.

The officers, naturally, were very dejected after their defeat. Long after the war one of them confessed that they were burdened with a sense of guilt for having failed to beat off the enemy assault, despite the impossible odds. There were some acrimonious exchanges between some of the officers for the failure, as some of them saw it, of others to pull their weight effectively during the enemy attack. Their CO, Colonel Carne, was so angry that he was not on speaking terms with some of his subordinates and is said to have severely reprimanded a few and reminded all the others of the standard of behaviour that he expected of them in captivity. When the going got rough for the officers, this reminder served to stiffen their resolve to acquit themselves of what some saw as their previous failures.

It took the Chinese many hours to round up over eight hundred British captives and when they did so they separated the officers and senior NCOs from the men. One of the men, Lance Corporal R. Mathews, related in a book that was written about his experiences in captivity:–

> It was a tense moment. We stood waiting, unable to understand the high-pitched agitation of the Chinese. The yellow men walked across to us with unexpected smiles. . . . We shook hands all round . . . there was no trace of hostility. They seemed so glad to see us. We learned later that it was not so much good will as good discipline that inspired the Chinese to spare our lives.

All the prisoners were searched and relieved of their weapons and their personal possessions, some of which disappeared before they could be returned. They were also relieved of their cigarettes which were placed in a heap and later redistributed.

By April the Chinese had created a marginally better system for dealing with p.o.w. than the chaos that had followed the capture of the January prisoners, although they were still experiencing difficulty in finding their way round the Korean countryside and were very dependent on the North Koreans, including the resentful civilian population, for overnight accommodation. After the Imjin River battle they established collecting points south of the river and routed small parties of p.o.w. through these to at least two Divisional 'cages' which had been established twenty miles north of the river. Several Chinese POW Guard Companies appeared and were deployed at intervals along the evacuation route to relay the prisoners from one transit camp to another. In January the Chinese had used North Korean troops for this purpose. With the hand-over to Guard Companies came a higher proportion of veteran P.O.W. Corps officers whose activities resulted in a more systematic attack on the morale, discipline and command structure of the British prisoners.

Because the evacuation took place in the spring and early summer it was possible to live out in the open without extreme hardship and offered better opportunities for escape. The spring weather also made it feasible for the prisoners to live off the land, though few had the necessary knowledge of edible weeds, an omission that was to cost them dearly. They were often short of water and scooped some from the paddyfields that had been manured with human and animal excrement, with dire results. Survival knowledge would have done much to alleviate the worst effects of malnutrition. Another very serious omission on the part of many prisoners was to divest themselves of their equipment, including, in some cases, their mess tins, an act they were soon bitterly to regret when food was handed out and they had nothing to collect it in.

Although too much must not be made of the milder weather, compared with the winter sufferings of the January captives it did make for a more rapid recovery of the prisoners' morale from the paralysing shock of capture. This again made for better discipline, better individual and group relationships, closer social integration and ultimately better co-ordinated action in defence of their elementary rights as prisoners of war.

The story of the evacuation of the main body of prisoners in two columns is again essentially one of a struggle for survival. It was also a struggle with the Chinese to maintain their traditional British command structure and organization. It began at the Divisional collecting points where they were greeted by representatives of the Prisoner of War Corps. Without mincing their words the Chinese informed their captives that they were now prisoners of the Chinese People's Volunteers; that they were war criminals and that ranks and seniorities were abolished and would no longer be recognized. Any prisoner attempting to exercise the authority of his rank would be punished. All prisoners were to obey the rules and regulations, as yet unspecified, and escaping was an offence punishable by death. The prisoners were told that they would be marched to the safe rear, though no mention was made of the distances involved.

One party received a thirty-minute speech in Chinese from a District Political Officer which took the interpreter two minutes to translate into English. It was a welcoming address loaded with politics, ending on a note of caution. Obey the rules and regulations, otherwise you will be shot. Other prisoners were handed slips of paper promising security of life, good treatment and a speedy evacuation to the safe rear. Yet others were handed propaganda pamphlets titled 'May We Be Heard', produced by British and American p.o.w. in the North Korean 'Peace Fighters' Camp' in Pyongyang.

When these preliminaries were completed the prisoners were divided into manageable groups irrespective of rank. They were then assembled into companies of a hundred prisoners, each of which was sub-divided into groups of ten equal squads. In each squad a prisoner, often the youngest, was detailed to be squad leader and was told that he was responsible for the behaviour of the men in his squad and would be shot if any of them attempted to escape. It proved to be an idle threat.

During a period of just over a week in the assembly area several other measures were taken to impose new behaviour patterns on the prisoners. Selected groups were harassed by Chinese political officers and interro-

1. George Blake, one of the first British subjects to be captured by the North Koreans. (Imperial War Museum).

2. Major M.D. Ryan of the Royal Ulster Rifles, the Senior British Officer of the January 1951 captives and one of the leaders of resistance to the Chinese. (Courtesy the Royal Ulster Rifles Association).

3. Captain (later Major General) James Majury of the Royal Ulster Rifles, one of the four officers to survive among the January 1951 captives. (Courtesy the Royal Ulster Rifles Association).

4. (above) A page from the diary kept by one of the January 1951 captives, believed to be Corporal W. Massey of the Royal Ulster Rifles, and (below) an enlargement of one of the pages.

5. The launching of the US – British POW Peace Organization by the Peace Fighters of Pyongyang. (North Korean Propaganda Picture).

6. Formation of Camp 5 Peace Committee in Pyoktong. (North Korean Propaganda Picture).

7. Lieut. Colonel J.P. Carne V.C. commanding officer of the 1st Battalion of the Gloucestershire Regiment, captured after the Imjin River battle, the most senior British officer held by the Chinese. (Imperial War Museum).

9. Major P.W. 'Sam' Weller of the Glosters, the Senior British Officer of the first column of Imjin River p.o.w. to reach Camp 1 on the Yalu River. (Courtesy of the Gloucestershire Regiment Museum).

8. Major E.D. Harding, second in command of the Glosters. (Courtesy the Gloucestershire Regiment Museum).

10. Captain (later General Sir Anthony) Farrar-Hockley, Adjutant of the Glosters who made many escape attempts and was tortured by the North Koreans. (Courtesy the Gloucestershire Regiment Museum).

11. Sergeant 'Bill' Sykes of the Glosters, one of the many p.o.w. punished by the Chinese for his 'hostile attitudes'. (Courtesy the Gloucestershire Regiment Museum).

12. Fusilier Derek Kinne, GC of the Royal Northumberland Fusiliers, tortured repeatedly by the Chinese for his many acts of defiance. (Courtesy D.G. Kinne).

13. Sketch showing the intermingling of Chinese and p.o.w. accommodation to segregate prisoner groups with the minimum of guards. Based on information of Camp 1 layout. (John Cunningham).

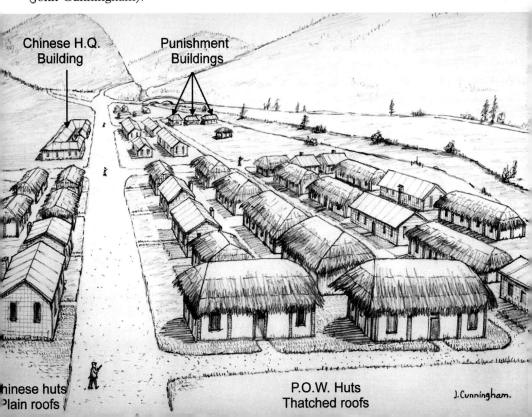

Chinese H.Q. Building

Punishment Buildings

Chinese huts Plain roofs

P.O.W. Huts Thatched roofs

J. Cunningham.

14. Sketch by the late Major Guy Ward, RA, of a house used to accommodate officer p.o.w. in Camp 2 (1). (By permission of Mrs. E. Ward).

15. Sketch of the inside of a p.o.w. hut in Camp 2 (1). (By permission of Mrs. E. Ward).

16. Sketch of the cookhouse in Camp 2 (1) which catered for 300 p.o.w. (By permission of Mrs. E. Ward).

17. Two items of enemy propaganda, the larger circulated at Communist 'Peace' Congresses, the smaller sent to the Next of Kin of British and American p.o.w. (C. Cunningham).

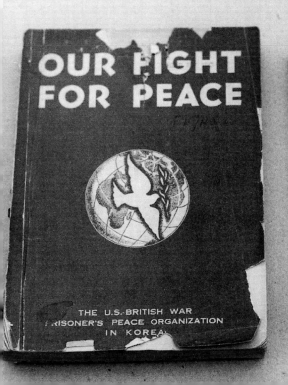

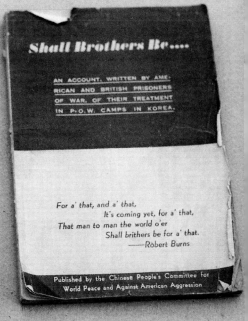

18. The author and his wife Mary in their flat in Reading where, over breakfast, officers of the Intelligence Corps were briefed for the de-briefing of the 'Little Switch' sick and wounded p.o.w at Tidworth Military Hospital. Inset: The author dressed as an Army officer to escape the attentions of the Press at Tidworth. (C. Cunningham).

19. The Gate of Freedom for the general release from captivity of United Nations p.o.w. in August 1953. (Imperial War Museum).

gators and produced the first clash between the British officers and their captors. Colonel Carne and several of his officers were singled out for questioning and when they refused to answer except to give the traditional response of name, rank and number they were punished in various ways. Colonel Carne was informed that the Chinese People's Volunteers could no longer supply him or his officers with any food. Not that they had received much in the way of food; they considered themselves fortunate to receive a daily handful of millet. It turned out to be another idle threat, but the rations of all the prisoners were barely enough to keep them alive. Several officers were insulted in front of their men; some were threatened with revolvers, others were made to stand to attention for hours on end and some were flung into holes in the ground to reflect upon their 'hostile attitudes'. The struggle for control had barely begun; the Chinese were still pussyfooting at this stage.

The interrogators made further attempts to gain information. Most prisoners were issued with a 'P.W. Registration Form', a questionnaire demanding all kinds of personal and military information, not unlike the autobiographical inventories that had been issued to the Marines at Kanggye. The men were at a loss to know how to react; some filled them in and others looked to their superiors for a lead, via the bush telegraph. The officers filled in their number, rank and name and drew their pencils through the rest of the questions. This made the Chinese hopping mad; they brandished their weapons and shouted at the culprits, who calmly ignored their threats despite being slapped and kicked. But some of the ORs were subjected to ill-treatment and several of those who refused to co-operate were treated according to the advice given by a senior officer of the P.O.W. Corps after the Kanggye experiment. They were broken by ruthless interrogation into informing on their peers and superiors, thus beginning the pernicious penetration of the social structure of every single prisoner group.

While these attacks were being made by the interrogators, the indoctrinators began their own insidious business. Captain Dain, a gunner, and the Regiment's padre, the Rev. S.J. Davies (the only U.N. Forces padre to survive captivity) and many other prisoners of all ranks were taken aside for political indoctrination. Also small groups of ORs were taken aside for friendly chats to sound out their political sympathies and their true opinions of their superiors. In this way the Chinese began pinpointing the disgruntled men and compiling dossiers.

The objective of most of these indoctrination and interrogation efforts was not to obtain military information but to identify actual and natural leaders and to collect information on every single prisoner's attitudes and background for their dossiers. Ninety per cent of the prisoners were asked for, and many gave, information on their relationships with their superiors, their own backgrounds and those of their friends and acquaintances.

During the stay at the Divisional area they had received little food and had witnessed or suffered beatings and noticed the enemy's callous indifference to the fate of individuals, all of which was scarcely consistent with the Chinese repeated promises of leniency. Few had any illusions about their future treatment and they became restless and began to test the Chinese security measures to see how far they could go, gauging the possibilities of escape. But on the whole they were too weak and exhausted to stand much chance of success, quite apart from the problem of concealing their occidental size and facial appearance among the oriental native population. Nevertheless, despite the risk, especially the risk of falling into the hands of North Korean troops, a number of them did have a go.

One of the first prisoners to take off was Farrar-Hockley. He had escaped soon after capture, as had Privates Fox and Graham of the Glosters, and an unknown number of others who had slipped away when the chances of regaining friendly lines were greatest. Farrar-Hockley was at liberty for three days and had reached a place near to where he had been captured after the Imjin River battle when he had the misfortune to walk into a North Korean army encampment. He was reasonably well treated by his captors for several days, during which he met up again with Fox and Graham who had also been recaptured by the North Koreans. While the trio were being marched from camp to camp they all managed to escape again, only to be recaptured by the Chinese.

From the Divisional transit camp two lieutenants of the Glosters, Henry Cabrael and Guy Temple, and the unit's medical officer, Bob Hickey, slipped away. Captain Hickey had long since been unable to practise his profession; from the very beginning the Chinese had robbed him of all his medical equipment and supplies and had refused him access to the sick and wounded. The trio made several attempts without success. Later Henry Cabrael died from ill treatment.

After leaving the Divisional area several more prisoners escaped, including Fusilier Derek Kinne of the Royal Northumberland Fusiliers, but there was little hope of success, since by now they were too far behind enemy lines.

Of all these escapers only two regained friendly lines due to the chaos and confusion behind the enemy's lines and the muddle that existed between the North Koreans and the Chinese People's Volunteers over the custody of escapers and splinter groups of p.o.w. Privates Fox and Graham were the luckiest men of the entire war. Fox was a young volunteer, a Liverpudlian. Graham, an older man, was an experienced recalled reservist, a dour north-countryman with a red beard. After repeatedly escaping and at one stage being sheltered by an elderly Korean woman, they somehow managed to avoid the wrath that their captors usually heaped upon escapers. Between their escape attempts they spent weeks being passed from one enemy unit to another and from North Korean to Chinese custody. Ultimately they had the amazing good fortune to be repatriated by the Chinese in compliance with the peculiarity of their Lenient Policy that impelled them to send some prisoners back through the front lines loaded with surrender leaflets and propaganda pamphlets! Fox and Graham brought with them some of the first reliable information on the enemy's treatment of British prisoners of war.

Shortly before the main bodies of prisoners left the Divisional areas for the journey to the Yalu River each squad received several heavy bags of food containing altogether a hundred and fifty pounds of rice. This was the rations for ten men for a month, about half a pound per man per day. The journey to Munhari, the last of the transit camps, was much the same as it had been for the January column. They marched by night, often in single file along the tops of dykes between the paddy fields, two hours' marching and ten minutes' rest. Many prisoners died from dysentery, malnutrition, respiratory diseases and unattended wounds. Those who were too sick to march were left behind and fell into the hands of the North Koreans. By the time the main body reached Munhari, sometimes called Halfway House, every single p.o.w. was seriously undernourished and all were suffering from diseases of one kind or another as a result of exposure and dirty, overcrowded quarters into which they had been herded overnight. As Fusilier Kinne recorded in his book *The Wooden Boxes*, "the old mucking-in spirit seemed to have disappeared" and selfishness began to prevail. Now they only helped their closest friends and individuals no longer shared their troubles. According to Kinne self-discipline had broken down and nearly all the ORs endeavoured to get extra food at the expense of their companions. Nevertheless self-interest never reached anything like the extremes that occurred among the American p.o.w. earlier in the year.

The officers closed ranks and steadfastly refused to abandon their normal standards of behaviour, setting a good example to their subordinates. Of them Kinne wrote, "I saw them in a new light, as if I

81

suddenly realized that all the fancy ways an officer had gave him something worthwhile to keep him going." One extraordinary example of the maintenance of their social mores occurred when Captain Bob Hickey operated without anaesthetics on Farrar-Hockley's infected feet with a razor blade after the latter's return from one of his escape attempts. Colonel Carne excused himself from the group holding down the struggling patient so that they could use as much bad language as they pleased!

The Chinese were well aware of the example the officers' behaviour was setting to their men and returned to their attack at Munhari. Colonel Carne and his second-in-command, Denis Harding, were subjected to a favourite Chinese form of torture. They had their hands tied behind their backs and were then suspended by their wrists from an overhanging beam for two hours. Captain Hickey, Captain Dain and several sergeants, including Sergeant Sharp of the Royal Northumberland Fusiliers and Sergeant Sykes of the Glosters, had their hands and arms tightly bound with wire and were flung into foxholes to reflect upon their 'hostile attitudes'. They had refused to give any military information and refused to confess in public to their 'crimes'. Sykes was being punished for smashing his own wrist watch to prevent it being looted by a Chinese guard. Captain Dain and Sergeant Sharp were left in their holes to foul themselves for a month in rainy weather and were left behind when the columns moved out of Munhari.

By the time the two columns reached their destination at Chongsong on 23 May and 9 June 1951 one hundred and thirty prisoners had perished in transit, which lent little credence to Chinese promises of leniency and good treatment. During the evacuation the Chinese had discovered to which platoon, company and regiment most of the prisoners belonged and were well informed of the identities and functions of key prisoners, such as Intelligence personnel, technical and signal specialists, snipers, former parachutists and fol-boat operators. They had also succeeded in persuading an unknown number of the prisoners to act as informers against those with 'hostile attitudes'.

8

THE SIMMERING POT

(Camp 1)

One of the principal lessons emerging from the history of the prisoners at Camp 5 at Pyoktong was that their early compliance was primarily due to their weakened condition due to their long winter march to a camp run by the North Koreans whose policy did indeed make the Chinese appear lenient by comparison. Another was that political exploitation of the main body of prisoners depended very largely upon the early identification and removal of unauthorized leaders, the so-called reactionaries, including the officers and senior NCOs from among the ORs, to prevent them from upsetting the political education of the majority or taking action against the hard-core progressives.

The situation at Camp 1 at Chongsong was very different. Almost from the moment of the arrival of p.o.w. from the Imjin River battle it became a simmering pot of resentment against the enemy. For one thing there were more officers and senior NCOs among the prisoners to maintain the chain of command at the early stages of captivity. But after their removal the potential reactionaries learned by painful trial and error that overt acts simply led to their own immediate removal, neutralizing any benefits that might have accrued from their leadership had they been more subtle, by inventing various unattributable ways of expressing their resentment. Nevertheless, as we shall see, their fumbling and uncoordinated acts of resistance significantly retarded the indoctrination programme, thereby interfering with the system by which the progressives were to be manoeuvred into positions of influence to gain control of the social structure and police the activities of the other prisoners. But not before the Chinese had wrung some political benefits from the reluctant compliance of the majority.

The Chongsong camp itself was in a pleasant locality some miles from the war-torn town from which it took its name. It comprised about two hundred mud and wattle huts on the south bank of a stream in vegetated foothills backed by mountains and was already occupied by American prisoners. There were no static defences, only a few guards stationed at strategic points, and yet, according to the Americans, nobody had succeeded in escaping. And as at Pyoktong, the camp had not yet been fully taken over by the Chinese.

The first column of three hundred British p.o.w., including men of the Glosters under Major P.W. Weller, reached the camp at the end of May and discovered that it was already occupied by six hundred American enlisted men living miserably in compounds run by thieves and racketeers, military discipline having broken down almost completely. They were regularly carrying their dead, two hundred in two months, to a cemetery on a hillside behind the camp, which they had dubbed 'Boot Hill'. A huge negro prisoner habitually emptied the pockets of the dead before they left for the cemetery and stowed their possessions in his kitbag for trading with other prisoners or with the enemy. He was but one of the racketeers who seemed to flourish among the Americans whose behaviour the British soldiers found profoundly shocking.

The new arrivals were divided up into squads, platoons and companies in the same way as the January column had been organized at Pyoktong. Each squad was allocated one room in a house, giving about a yard of space to each man. Empty rice sacks served as ground sheets and each roomful of prisoners was given three old overcoats as bedclothes.

After the long march there was a strong urge to relax, but Weller realized that if he did not take command the behaviour of the British p.o.w. would probably deteriorate to the level of the Americans. He went the rounds of his men, discreetly reminding them of their responsibilities as soldiers and their duty to maintain the chain of command. He pointed out that it was in their own interests to clean up their quarters and to arrange for the fair distribution of food and duties. He made numerous useful suggestions as to how best to utilize their primitive accommodation and facilities. He taught some how to identify and prepare nutritious edible weeds that grew in profusion near the camp. He also called for volunteers to fill in old latrines and dig new ones. Although he exercised his authority discreetly he was well aware of the risks he was taking and the danger of being charged with 'plotting and organizing a conspiracy', which, as all the prisoners had been told, carried a death sentence or imprisonment for life. In due course he had to face these and other charges.

According to one eye witness, Weller got away with it for about two weeks before the Chinese pounced. There were a number of British prisoners who resented being put to work, who preferred to relax and adopt

84

the attitude that for them the war was over. One such man worked under protest in the cookhouse and one day went on strike. Weller approached him and endeavoured to make him modify his behaviour and when the soft approach failed issued him with a direct order. A snooping Chinese officer overheard the command. Weller was arrested and escorted to the camp H.Q. where he was informed that by 'intimidating' a fellow prisoner he had committed a serious offence. He was cautioned and reminded that he was no longer permitted to exercise his rank and was allowed to return to his compound. Two days later he disappeared.

The sudden disappearance of their implacable leader was an ominous reminder to all who held any rank that they would not be allowed to exercise their authority. They were permitted to believe that he had been shot but in fact he had been transferred to another, heavily guarded compound further up the road. But he had left his mark and had kindled some spirit in the British prisoners. It was this early spirit and mounting resentment at the two-faced treatment they had experienced on the march, with Chinese promises of leniency negated by brutal punishment for petty infractions, which marked the difference between the ORs at Chongsong and those at Pyoktong. The latter had only four officers among their number and were in a much worse physical condition when they reached Pyoktong. It is therefore not surprising that a greater proportion of them turned to the only quarter that could offer them some stability and a chance of survival, the Chinese.

On 9 June the second, larger British column, headed by Colonel Carne, arrived in the camp. Every day for the next few weeks all prisoners were compelled to attend political lectures given by Chinese political officers who were so ill-versed in their topics that they invited booing and catcalls. Their incompetence spilled over into the discussions of set questions where the speakers were frequently challenged on a variety of elementary issues about their Dickensian visions of life under capitalism. But the lecture periods were not without some advantage because it brought all the prisoners together and provided Colonel Carne and his team of nearly forty officers with the opportunity to keep in touch with their men and pass on advice and encouragement.

For the Chinese, however, the presence of the British officers in the Anglo-American audience was a source of continuous irritation. The mere presence of Colonel Carne, who at this stage was the most senior officer in the camp, had a disciplinary effect on all ranks; his prestige was as high among the Americans as it was among his own countrymen. Moreover, the British officers did not allow the Chinese political assertions to go unchallenged. And they had the disconcerting habit of asking awkward questions at the lecture assemblies with a persistence and character that suggested a well-organized conspiracy, setting a very 'bad' example to the other ranks. Worse, from the Chinese point of view, it caused them to lose a considerable amount of 'face'. Such disadvantages could not long be tolerated.

It is uncertain when the prisoners were required to elect their Daily Life Committees to organize the running of the camp, whether it was after the arrival of Colonel Carne and the second column or in July after the full implementation of the Lenient Policy. What is known is that in June and July all the prisoners, including the officers and NCOs, were subjected to intensive political lectures and study groups by an incompetent team of indoctrinators, in the same way as they had been in Pyoktong. And, as at Pyoktong, the prisoners quickly learned to delegate the note-taking to one of their number while the rest slept or amused themselves. Lectures were followed with the issue of questions to be discussed by each squad and again for a while the prisoners got away with delegating the work to one of their number while the rest played cards or similar games. But not for long. If the squad failed to return an acceptable (i.e. Communist) answer, which was often, a political officer descended upon the squad, making individual participation unavoidable, and kept them arguing and discussing through mealtimes, causing missed meals or long delays in the delivery of food which, when it came, was half-rations. The squads soon learned not to argue and to compile acceptable answers. However, the tuition evidently did not produce sufficient potential progressives, as it had done at the equivalent stage in Pyoktong. The Chongsong prisoners seem to have been slow learners, which led to a dearth of progressives and so prevented the Chinese from loading the camp's domestic organizations with their preferred candidates. They were obliged to allow a number of British ORs of dubious political attitudes to take office in various camp organizations, thereby granting opportunities which some of the less impetuous reactionaries were quick to take. The result was that the job of Chairman of the Daily Life Committee in the ORs compound was taken by Corporal Frank Upjohn of the Glosters who now held a position equal to that of Marine Andrew Condron in Pyoktong. Unlike Condron, however, Upjohn was a wily reactionary. Initially he seems to have been uncertain as to how to exploit his position and his plans at this stage are obscure. It was to be some months before he made any moves to use his position to advantage and later to use it as a cover for assisting escapes. In the meantime he contented himself with using it to make regular visits

86

to the Chinese camp HQ, where he inspected their records in an attempt to find out which of his fellow prisoners could be trusted. He must have been thwarted if the records were kept in Chinese script and therefore he probably obtained his information by discussions with the Chinese to sound out their preferences of personnel. Actually, he was not the only one to be doing some amateur sleuthing. Unbeknown to him, and to each other, Corporal W.K. Westwood of the Glosters and Lance Corporal G. McLaughlin of the Royal Ulster Rifles were indulging in similar activities, making their own investigations into who was aiding the enemy and who was not. Westwood, a 'K' Volunteer, was the modern equivalent of a gentleman ranker who had formerly served in the Intelligence Corps and was to return to the Corps after repatriation. When all three were ultimately discovered by their captors they were indicted on serious charges. The Chinese refused to believe that they had acted upon their own initiatives and branded them as secret agents in an organized plot.

It is perhaps appropriate at this point to mention that the Chinese were very well aware of the part played by M.I.9 in running escape lines during the Second World War. They were also aware of its organization among British p.o.w. within German camps. They were constantly on the lookout for evidence of its existence and operation in Korea and constantly re-squadded prisoners as one of its countermeasures. In fact M.I.9 had not been re-activated, in the form of A.I.9, until it was too late to be of any use to those who were captured in January and April of 1951. More to the point, it did *not* run any escape lines in Korea and did not even organize any kind of escape or resistance activity within the p.o.w. camps. Its role was almost entirely humanitarian and the collection of P.O.W. Intelligence.

Early in July the Chinese seem to have taken full control of the camp and brought in a staff of seventy-six political indoctrinators, half of whom could speak tolerable English. A new regime was introduced to fully implement their Lenient Policy. The British officers were transferred to what amounted to a reactionary compound, to the one in which Weller was living with recalcitrant American officers. This move was followed by the re-mustering of the sergeants, previously scattered among the squads of other ranks, into their own reactionary platoons in a separate part of the compound, to prevent them exerting their 'bad' influence. This left only prisoners of the rank of corporal and below in the ORs' compound. As a first step the ORs were divided into two companies each of about three hundred prisoners who were then accommodated in separate compounds to facilitate better control. As at Pyoktong, each company was now divided into three platoons of ten squads, with about a dozen prisoners in each squad, to which was attached a Chinese political officer. Then, one or two men from each squad, usually the youngest or those already showing progressive tendencies, were detailed to attend classes every morning for the next three weeks to adjust their attitudes and train them for the job of squad leaders, to which positions they were appointed on returning to their squads, regardless of the wishes of the men whose quarters they shared. Their tasks was to act as overt informers on the members of their squads and check that none of them were missing. But, as one British soldier put it, when the squad leaders returned to their squads they were faced with a dozen or so men who set about the task of diluting their attitudes and encouraging them, as only a seasoned ranker knows how, by veiled threats or accidental mishaps, to be careless in the execution of their duties.

The prisoners were about to be introduced to some of the benefits of the Lenient Policy. One British soldier estimated that there were seventy-six Chinese political officers on the staff of a political commissar who took precedence over the military camp commandant. Half of the political staff spoke good English. Previously the task had been performed by a scratch team with little knowledge of the political situation in Great Britain and evidently little knowledge of group dynamics. From here on leadership within the ORs' compounds would depend either upon those who could be converted into progressives and rewarded with authority by the Chinese or upon the emergence of strong natural leaders who were smart enough to conceal that they were steering from the rear. The scene was set for a tussle that had no parallel at Pyoktong.

July and August were months of intensive political indoctrination coinciding with the opening of the Peace Talks at Kaesong and was intended to use the prisoners to put pressure on the U.N. negotiators to agree to peace on Communist terms. The strategic objective was to get the prisoners to produce a huge volume of propaganda praising the cause of their captors and discrediting the 'capitalists'. It was to be unleashed worldwide through the media and various influential Communist 'front' organizations. But, unlike the easy compliance that the Chinese had achieved at Pyoktong, the immediate effect in Chongsong was to create widespread resentment among the prisoners at having politics rammed down their throats all day long and at having their genuine opinions stifled. Unfortunately it spurred the reactionaries into action. It permitted them to identify the genuine progressives because of the sincerity of their political interests and led to their victimization by acts of revenge. This, in turn, permitted the Chinese to identify the impetuous reactionaries by their 'hostile acts' and spurred the camp security staff to accelerate its insidious business of inducting informers by threats and savage punishments and infiltrating them into the squads, especially those considered to be 'reactionary'. Thus the first, overt, moves made by the reactionaries played directly into the hands of the Chinese.

In July, just as the reorganization was taking place, an escape attempt had been made by Sergeant S.J. Brisland and Corporal L. Charman, both of the Glosters. They were at liberty for three days and upon recapture were paraded before the assembled prisoners to make their confessions. When these proved inadequate they were sentenced to sixteen days in a Korean jail to help them to 'realize their errors'. In jail they were compelled to squat motionless for sixteen hours each day and were beaten with sticks by the Korean guards if they slouched or moved to ease the cramp in their legs. After a week they were visited by a Chinese officer who asked if they had seen the error of their ways and when they asked him what he meant they were kept in jail for another week. At the end of the second week they said they now realized their errors and were taken back to the camp to make their 'sincere' confessions, repenting for their 'war crimes', expressing their remorse and ingratitude and apologizing for their 'hostile attitudes'. Brisland's confession, tongue in cheek, was a classic, long remembered by those who heard it. Liberally laced with Communist jargon, it incorporated a wealth of valuable escape information about conditions outside the camp. He had been caught, he said, by a sharp-eyed Korean boy who had reported him to the police. He inferred rather than said that bridges should be avoided and one should wade or swim across streams. He mentioned that he had been unable to cook his dried rice, inferring that he had forgotten his matches, and again, by inference, suggested it was better to try and live off the land by stealing food from the locals, if one could. It all sailed over the heads of the beaming Chinese until they heard the prolonged and vociferous cheers of the assembled p.o.w at the end of his performance. Charman's confession was in the same vein but less polished. Immediately afterwards the pair were sentenced to seven days' hard labour. Henceforth the Chinese invariably sought a double meaning in just about everything the prisoners did and said.

The next confrontation came over the issue of autobiographical inventories which the Chinese required the squad leaders to distribute to each member of their squads. Many of them refused to do so, but this obstinacy was overcome by the simple ruse of telling the ORs that Colonel

Carne had completed his. It was a lie, but the trick worked. However, the manner in which many of the ORs filled in their inventories displeased the Chinese and many of the prisoners refused to sign the completed forms. The Chinese always insisted on the prisoners signing documents in case they tried to retract later. On this occasion some of the prisoners were adamant. They included Corporal A. Holdam, MM, Privates N.E.S. Godden and K Godwin and others who received decorations for their resistance activities after they were repatriated. It is not known whether the Chinese took immediate action against them but from this time onwards they became targets of every informer in their compounds.

The compulsory lectures and study periods dragged on with ever-increasing overt and covert opposition. Evidently the indoctrination of the prisoners still had not yielded sufficient progressives to allow adequate political control. In July the prisoners were ordered to send a telegram of greetings to the Communist-sponsored Chicago Peace Conference. The officers and sergeants refused to have anything to do with the scheme, but the ORs were duped into signing by telling them that the Chicago Peace Conference was a non-political meeting of religious and philanthropic organizations. A telegram was sent on behalf of *all* the prisoners in Camp 1, despite the intransigence of the officers and sergeants.

On 1 August all the prisoners were issued with notebooks to facilitate their political studies and some of them made the grave error of using these, and old copies of the *Shanghai News*, for toilet paper or for rolling cigarettes. Immediately there were savage reprisals against the culprits for "destroying the people's property".

One night, during a bed check, a Chinese guard startled Gunner M.E. Dunnachie, who sat up suddenly and sent the guard sprawling through the door of his hut. He was immediately arrested and removed to a cell where he was ordered to confess to assaulting the guard. When he said it was an accident, he was kicked into a squatting position and beaten about the head and body and threatened with a loaded pistol. When he still insisted that it was an accident, his hands were tied behind his back and the running end of the rope was thrown over a beam, shortened, forcing his hands up his back, compelling him to teeter on tiptoe. The loose end of the rope was then noosed about his neck so that if he tried to relieve the agony in his arms he would hang himself. When this failed to elicit a confession he was flung into solitary confinement in a Korean cell without a toilet and regularly beaten up until he agreed to confess. He was paraded before the entire camp to confess his 'crimes'. He also had to give a public guarantee of his future good behaviour and express his willingness to accept any punishment that the Chinese might see fit to impose should he break his word.

Shortly after this incident Private R.G. Shelton of the Glosters was accused by his captors of stealing soap. Although innocent, he was arrested, imprisoned and beaten up until he agreed to confess to "stealing the people's property".

Clearly the Chinese were getting jumpy and did not seem to realize that with every punishment they were meting out they were negating their promises of Leniency and contradicting their own propaganda about the glories and social justice of Communism. The ORs were becoming increasingly resentful and uncooperative. They had stepped up their heckling at lectures and returned study questions unanswered or provocatively phrased. Several of the more prominent progressives were beaten up by a group of British p.o.w. calling themselves the 'execution' squad. Some of the progressives were ceremonially de-bagged and had had their naked posteriors and private parts daubed with indelible dye stolen from the Chinese sick quarters. Another group started psychological warfare against actual and suspected progressives by plastering the compound with posters warning them of the penalties for treason. Overnight pictures of Mao Tse-tung acquired Hitler moustaches, to the fury of the Chinese. The artists in these escapades were Lance Corporal Sharpling and Private Ward of the Glosters and the poster-hanger was Fusilier Derek Kinne who had already started his private war against the Chinese by sneaking into the cookhouse and dosing their food with D.D.T. and powdered glass.

In the middle of August three more men of the Glosters, Lance Corporal K. Newby and Privates R. Stockting and 'Geordie' Dawson, attempted to escape. They were quickly recaptured and thrown into prison until they 'realized their errors'. Once again their escape had been an act of desperation, though the Chinese regarded it as gross ingratitude for the Leniency they had been shown.

Addressing all the assembled prisoners, including the officers and sergeants, at the compulsory lectures the following morning the Camp Commandant reminded them that past warnings had been for their own safety. It was, he said, unbelievable that anyone should try to escape and he went on to outline yet again the virtues of the Lenient Policy and why the prisoners should be eternally grateful for having their lives spared after committing war crimes. They were lucky to be alive and should appreciate the chance they were being given to study the truth until they could go home. In the meantime they must be friends of the Chinese and no longer adopt hostile attitudes. They must learn to repent and learn the

91

meaning of peace. Escape was impossible and the Koreans could not be blamed if they killed escapers. His speech was recorded verbatim by one of the prisoners. He continued:–

> Don't be duped by rumour mongers. The American monopoly capitalists are trying to sabotage the Peace Talks, including recently trying to get the demarcation line thirty to forty miles inside Chinese and North Korean territory. By comparison the Chinese and North Koreans originated the peace proposals, including the exchange of prisoners.

He concluded with a warning:–

> The Lenient Policy is unchangeable, but there must be no sabotage of study or trouble-making over study. A hostile attitude to study or attempts to spoil other students' study will be punished. Concentrate on study and don't try to escape. If you are friendly to us, you will be treated as a friend, but the Lenient Policy has its limitations as regards our enemies.

Newby, Stockting and Dawson were by now fully aware of the limitations of the Lenient Policy. They were in jail where the Korean guards took a delight in beating them up with long sticks and making them stand motionless on one leg until they dropped and received another beating. This was in preparation for the inevitable confessions. But the Chinese were in no hurry. The process dragged on for a month, awaiting an opportunity to use their public confessions with telling effect against the recalcitrant majority.

In the middle of August the thorny subject of forming Peace Committees was raised. These had been formed two months previously in Pyoktong. But in Chongsong the Chinese failed to find a sufficient number of prisoners to stand for election.

Yet on 29 August the Camp Commandant had the effrontery to congratulate all the prisoners on their 'progress' during the month. That same day Private D.C. Richards of the Glosters had refused to study any more and had been dragged off to the local Korean jail where he stayed for twenty-seven days, receiving numerous sound beatings for producing five caustic self-criticisms. On his return to the camp, he was placed into a reactionary platoon which had been formed in his absence.

On 25 September the Chinese ordered the prisoners to elect Peace

Committees by 1 October and announced that their inauguration would be celebrated simultaneously with their National Day. But, the announcement added, officers would not be allowed to take part in these elections as 'punishment for their past reactionary activities'. Nothing was said about the increasing reactionary activities in the ORs compounds where no less than thirteen escape attempts had been made by British and American prisoners in the past two months.

All these escapers, including Newby, Stockting and Dawson, were now in jail and were dragged before the entire camp to make their confessions at an 'Anti-Escape Meeting'. The timing was significant, as usual. The meeting was intended to deter not only escape attempts but also to remind the prisoners of what would happen if they failed to comply with the order to form Peace Committees. But the British trio and one of the Americans upset the plans to make examples of them. They refused to show remorse for their 'errors' and once again used their confessions to pass to the assembly vital escape information on conditions outside the camp. Immediately afterwards the escapers were sentenced to fifteen days' hard labour and were sent back to jail for 'further education'.

On passing the sentences the Camp Commandant added:–

These are light punishments based upon the People's Army policy of educating people out of their mistakes. If you think it worthwhile to try to escape, remember the Chinese proverb that enjoins one to avoid anything which leads to punishment. You have been tools of warmongers. Therefore the Lenient Policy applies to you. But bad students, those who are against peace, and escapers will be treated differently. Why try criminal methods of returning home? The best you can hope for is to be sent back to camp. It is impossible to succeed. Stay and have a happy life in camp. The good students study to fight for peace. Spend a happy winter here in studying the truth! A Peace Committee is to be organized by 1 October, and you should prepare recreations for that day and learn songs and prepare plays. Wine has arrived to celebrate the occasion!

The return of the escapers to jail and further ill-treatment was to have a dreadful sequel when the prisoners were repatriated. Newby committed suicide on the troopship carrying him home. He left a cryptic message addressed to M.I.5. on a cigarette packet, along with a letter showing that he believed he had contracted a serious disease. The message turned out to be meaningless and a post-mortem carried out on board the troopship showed that he was not diseased. Such was the price he paid for his desperate courage.

The last few days of September were spent in feverish preparation for the 1 October celebrations and with electioneering for the Peace Committees. On the 28th the Chinese announced that a mass rally would be held as part of the celebrations and the prisoners were told that they would be required to parade with banners and suitable slogans and would march past high-ranking Chinese officers. Materials were provided for the prisoners to make two hundred banners painted with Communist slogans.

The following day the Peace Committee elections began. The voting was supposed to be secret, yet each ballot paper was scrutinized by the Chinese before it was allowed to be placed in the ballot box. Even so, in the Sergeants' compound the box was filled with blank papers and the officers refused to participate.

On 30 September the prisoners were ordered to wash their clothes in preparation for the march-past. Competitive singing was arranged between Nos 1 and 4 companies. Needless to say they were all Communist songs. No Western tunes were permitted, partly because the Chinese feared that they would be patriotic songs (e.g. the National Anthem) or popular songs that would be used to ridicule them or would possess defamatory innuendo.

During the day the results of the Peace Committee bogus elections were chalked up on a blackboard by a British soldier who shall be called Judas, notorious for his duplicity. He posed as a progressive for purely personal gain and, while praising the Chinese to their faces to establish his 'sincerity', would curse them behind their backs. He was eventually betrayed by informers and condemned to a penal camp where he was regarded with extreme suspicion. Meantime he recorded his own name as the successful candidate as the President of Camp No. 1 Permanent Peace Committee; all the rest were leading progressives with the exception of Corporal Frank Upjohn who had somehow got himself elected. Judas was the most hated prisoner in the camp and his progressive associates were all utterly despised. In due course they were to be subjected to so much abuse by their fellow prisoners that they had to be removed to Pyoktong for their own safety and consequently their Peace activities were abruptly terminated after a much briefer life than its equivalent in Pyoktong.

It might be argued that, had more of the reactionaries been less impetuous and more wily like Upjohn, more of them might have got themselves elected to positions of responsibility within the camps, especially the Daily Life Committees, or at least gained these positions in sufficient numbers to neutralize the influence of the progressives. In the event the elected Peace Committee men were nowhere near the calibre of the Pyoktong Peace Committee.

However, the haphazard acts of resistance ultimately had the desired effect of curbing the Chinese political intentions and because they were haphazard had the advantage of making it exceedingly difficult for the Chinese to detect the opposition. They had to deal with the situation piecemeal.

October 1, Revolution Day, was a cause for great celebration and the promise of a feast, following a mass rally of prisoners carrying hundreds of banners daubed with Communist slogans. There was an air of expectancy about the camp and to the surprise of all the prisoners they were served with a superb breakfast and issued with a bonus of five cigarettes, a bribe for what the Chinese hoped would be their compliant behaviour. As one prisoner reported afterwards, it promised a day out, relief from their monotonous existence, a chance to let off steam and the reward of a banquet. So everybody decided to make it a day of entertainment and to give of their best in the parade. At the appointed hour several thousand British and American prisoners carrying hundreds of banners marched past the local Korean population and a group of high-ranking Chinese officers, bellowing at the tops of their voices such slogans as "We want Peace" or "Down with War", "Asia for the Asians", "Beer is Best", "Up Yours Too" (as they thrust their banners skywards), "Everton for the Cup", and "Peace for All". Some of the slogans referred to the heredity of the Chinese dignitaries. The demonstration was lavishly photographed by an army of photographers and recorded in imaginative detail by journalists from all the Communist countries and from a number of neutral countries. It is doubtful if any of the witnesses noticed that there were no British officers in the parade and only four British sergeants who bellowed their true feelings as they marched past.

That night, instead of being fed on their usual diet of boiled millet and sorghum and weevily rice, the participants received a decent meal of plenty of potatoes, boiled onions, an egg and a quantity of fish. They were also issued with another bonus of cigarettes and two fluid ounces of wine which one prisoner said tasted like petrol. The celebrations continued long after dark, with community singing, pre-arranged by Private W. Palfry to create a noisy diversion for an escape attempt by Corporal C. Bailey of the Glosters and Lance Corporal R. Mathews of the REME. They were away for three days and upon recapture were sent to join Newby, Stockting and Dawson in the local Korean jail.

There is no denying that the Revolution Day parade provided the Communists with propaganda of tremendous value because, although it was easy for the outside world to account for the political defection of a minority, there seemed to be only one reasonable explanation for the apparent enthusiasm of several thousand p.o.w. When the incident is considered in the context of a lack of proof of widespread Chinese ill-treatment of prisoners the heartburnings in London and Washington can well be imagined. It put immense pressure upon the U.N. negotiators to reach an agreement at the Peace Talks.

Sometime after the parade all the officers were removed from the camp, transferred to a new one exclusively for officers at Pin Chon-Ni, which became Camp 2 (Branch 1).

Although the Chinese would not allow the practise of religion in the camps, they allowed, indeed encouraged, the prisoners to celebrate Christmas in the traditional way in order to milk it for its propaganda value. The prisoners were allowed to set up and decorate Christmas trees and were allowed to have a religious service, a concert and carol singing. Some of the reactionaries were temporarily released from prison and on Christmas day all the prisoners were given a feast. They were all encouraged to send Christmas greetings to their relatives at home. One Chinese propaganda document, which carried eighteen large pictures of the celebrations (all taken in Camp 5), listed a menu comprising fried chicken, mashed potatoes, beef stew, apple turnovers, doughnuts, tomato catsup (sic) and bread, butter and jam. Once again all the celebration and feasting were lavishly photographed and spread around the outside world to support the Chinese claim of 'Leniency' and tolerance!

Early in January 1952 an assessment was made in A.I.9 of the 'progress' being made by the Chinese among the prisoners in Chongsong. The indications were that three of the ORs were collaborating in every way and a further seven were close to political defection. In addition twenty-three had engaged in minor political activities, giving a total of a mere five per cent who had succumbed in varying degrees after six months of political indoctrination. Clearly the Chinese strategy was failing to produce sufficient progressives to take over control of the camp. Against this, up to Christmas 1951, eighty-seven ORs, that is thirteen per cent, had been punished by their captors for their reactionary activities. It was to increase rapidly.

It became perfectly clear that the British ORs grossly underestimated the Chinese security arrangements. They were too trusting of their fellow prisoners and were unprepared for the extent to which their squads, even the reactionary squads, and platoons had been penetrated by informers. They were also being watched by the large number of Chinese on the camp staff. (One prisoner estimated that there was one Chinese to every three p.o.w.) Moreover they were very naïve conspirators. One of the escapers said that some of the escape groups were conspicuously conspiratorial and therefore open to routine counter-intelligence techniques. Although the reactionaries in Chongsong claimed upon repatriation that they had taken reasonable precautions to conceal their activities from the men they knew to be progressives these were grossly inadequate to protect them from the Chinese watchers, secret informers, *agents provocateurs* and possibly monitoring devices. Just how extensive the informer networks were in Chongsong will never be known, but, based upon information about their extent in Pyoktong, it is likely that every squad possessed at least one overt informer in the form of the squad leader or monitor and at least one man who had been secretly inducted. But of much greater danger to the organizers and participants in resistance and escape activity were two men, both accepted as established reactionaries, who were secretly working for the Chinese. The results were calamitous.

The escape groups which mushroomed in the camp in 1952 did not justify the titles of committees. They were all loose arrangements between friends and lacked any kind of central co-ordination and were without informed direction. There were at least four groups operating simultaneously and often against the interests of each other.

The story of the rash of escape attempts begins on New Year's Day when Upjohn made his first approach to Lance Corporal Mathews, recently released from jail after his first escape attempt. The meeting took place during a compulsory political lecture and the outcome was scarcely encouraging. Upjohn realized that there was a need for co-ordination in the collection of food and other resources for escape attempts, but warned Mathews that the Chinese were closely watching all the escapers and the matter was dropped. Three months later, in March, Upjohn made another approach and the pair assumed the task of co-ordination. They invited Private N.E.S. Godden of the Glosters to join them. Availing himself freely of the records that the Chinese apparently kept of all the possessions of prisoners, Upjohn sent two of his conspirators into the compounds to contact no fewer than sixty men for items that would be useful for escaping. They were helped by Lance Corporal R. Prior, Private T. Nugent and Marine P.D. Murphy. Godden, who had contacts in the cookhouse, arranged for the collection and husbanding of food and started making maps. These early moves did not escape the notice of many prisoners and, inevitably, neither did they go unnoticed by the Chinese.

Early in April three men of the Royal Ulster Rifles, Dunne, Moore and Kaye, who were planning to escape, contacted Mathews for assistance. Despite the vigilance of the Chinese guards the two groups managed to make a dump of essential supplies on the route which the trio intended to take out of the camp and a day or so later made their first attempt. Unfortunately, they forgot to include any matches and were forced to turn back and returned unseen.

That night several lorry-loads of Chinese troops moved into the camp and sealed off all but one of the routes into the hills. Both Upjohn and Mathews regarded this as a routine precaution that the Chinese were bound to take at the opening of the escaping season. They also judged that, as Dunne, Moore and Kaye had returned safely, their plans had not been compromised.

It is now certain that the Chinese had already launched a cunning plan to scotch once and for all what they believed to be a well-organized central escape committee. It had begun several days previously when a notorious progressive, a corporal in the Glosters who shall be known as Smee, approached Upjohn and asked him point-blank when the committee intended to start its operations. Smee was well known to be dangerous and had been living in comparative luxury in the Chinese HQ where he was engaged on extensive propaganda activities and other sleazy acts of co-operation. Nevertheless, he apparently managed to allay Upjohn's darkest suspicions by telling him that he, Smee, had been allowed to go for unescorted walks into the hills for some time, a fact well known to every prisoner in the camp. During one of his walks, Smee said, he had been approached by a Korean who produced documents identifying himself as an American secret agent. The agent had told him that if the escapers could reach a certain village fifty miles away they would be helped to regain United Nations lines by an underground escape organization.

To prisoners with knowledge of the escape lines that had existed in the Second World War, hoping that similar arrangements had been made in Korea, it all sounded very plausible and commanded the close attention of Upjohn and his associates. It gained credence from a recent rumour that Korean agents had been operating near the sergeants' compound further up the road. Unfortunately the escapers' dreams of an assisted passage were groundless and led them straight into a Chinese trap. Meanwhile, Upjohn took the precaution of having Smee watched for a week, but failed to discover any evidence of duplicity over and above what he knew already.

On 25 April Dunne, Moore and Kaye made their second escape attempt and were immediately caught and flung into prison. Mathews and several of his helpers were arrested and taken to the Chinese HQ, where they were briefly interrogated, cautioned and allowed to return to their huts. The next day the Chinese positioned machine guns round the camp, pointing inwards in anticipation of a mass break-out. (Aerial photographs taken at this time revealed the sudden appearance and positioning of these guns, raising alarm at what might be happening in the camp to justify their appearance and concern at the possibility of the mass murder of prisoners.)

The release of Mathews made it seem that the Chinese trap had been sprung prematurely, but it did not prevent the Chinese from setting it again in the hope of a bigger catch.

For a few weeks Upjohn and his associates remained dormant, considerably shaken by events. In blissful ignorance of what awaited them, they resumed their plotting early in May when Corporal A.A. Holdam and his party approached Upjohn and his men for assistance. Holdam was a short, blond, powerfully built young man who had won his MM during the Second World War for operating a wireless set for the SAS behind enemy lines, a fact that he had so far managed to conceal from his captors. It was considered that his experience gave him a far better chance of escape than any other prisoner in the camp, but, irrationally, he imperilled his party at the very outset by permitting himself to plan an escape based upon the information that had been obtained from Smee. Even worse, they took Smee into their confidence!

It was at this stage that others intent upon escaping became alarmed and formed another, rival group, under a soldier by the name of Conner (whose full name and rank is unfortunately unknown).

Actually, the Upjohn group was in a more precarious position than they imagined because one of Holdam's party, an accepted reactionary, had been planted on them by the Chinese security officers.

Holdam and his party left the camp on 14 May during an air raid and made for the rendezvous supplied by Smee. It was about 48 hours before the escape was discovered and then Upjohn, Mathews, Godden and two others, Corporal K. Walters and Private K. Godwin, were separately arrested. They were charged with "plotting and unlawful activities" and were arraigned before a formal Chinese tribunal. They all refused to confess and were convicted without a hearing. They were transferred to a penal compound on the periphery of the camp and spent the next six months in solitary confinement in a special prison where the cells were small bamboo cabins with earth floors within a larger building. They had no contact with each other, indeed they did not know if their compatriots were in the same prison. They were unable to wash themselves and were individually allowed out only to visit the toilet occasionally or to be hauled before an interrogator. They were not allowed to wash and only once were they taken, alone, to a river to wash their clothes and themselves because their tormentors could no longer bear the smell of them. They were visited periodically by a senior Chinese officer to see if they were prepared to confess. They refused. One day, as Mathews was returning from an interrogation, he saw Holdam in manacles, being led in the opposite direction. It was the first indication he had that the escape had failed. Demoralized by the failure, he began to make a limited confession which proved unacceptable. But still he refused to confess to organizing escapes and his exasperated interrogator reminded him that he had pushed the Lenient Policy beyond its limits and could therefore be executed. However, as the Chinese were not barbarians like the Americans, he would be moved to less comfortable quarters.

He was led across the compound to another building within which was what became known as the wooden boxes, not much bigger than dog kennels, five feet long and four feet wide and high, within which it was impossible to sit upright or to lay outstretched.

Holdam and his party had been at liberty for four days and had crossed twenty miles of country before their absence was discovered. On the second night out the informer in the party dropped out on the excuse that he would make his own way to United Nations lines, but the evidence indicated that he gave himself up in order to give the Chinese up-to-date information on Holdam's route and his intentions. The escape party avoided several ambushes that were laid across their route which alerted them to Smee's treachery and were able to elude their pursuers for two more days before they were ambushed by North Koreans. They were taken back to Chongsong and viciously interrogated before being transferred to the penal compound.

This ill-fated attempt upset the plans of several other groups preparing to escape and put the Chinese on their guard. Nevertheless, early in June Privates D.J. Green and P.J. Jordon and Gunner M. Menand, all of whom had received some help from Upjohn and his helpers, made an attempt to get away. Almost immediately Green was discovered, but the other two managed to return to their huts undetected. Green was forced to stand for

100

fourteen hours while being interrogated and afterwards was permitted to return to his compound where he was placed under close surveillance by the Chinese and their stool pigeons.

On 14 June Jordon, with two new companions, Privates H. Pemberton and G. Wood, made another attempt to escape and were at liberty for four days. On recapture they were handcuffed and consigned to the wooden boxes in the penal compound and afterwards were interrogated exhaustively for four days and nights. The Chinese were puzzled as to how the trio had managed to get sixty miles from the camp, a feat which they believed was impossible without outside assistance. Evidently they were still searching for escape lines similar to those run by M.I.9 in the Second World War. The trio were sentenced to three months' hard labour in the camp's hard labour unit and were released only when they gave written guarantees of their future good behaviour.

All the British prisoners sentenced to hard labour found ways of tormenting the Chinese who, when lacking purposeful heavy labour, set the prisoners to useless tasks like digging holes in the rocky ground and then filling them in. The prisoners retaliated by digging holes, conspiring ostentatiously while one of their number wrote something on a piece of paper, which was flung into the hole and rapidly covered with earth. The snooping Chinese compelled them to unearth the secret message and hand it over. It read "Mind your own business" or some other stinging remark!

Undaunted by the annihilation of the Upjohn group and its escape parties, Conner and his group made preparations which matured in the middle of June when a party of five, Gunners M. Menand and R. Thompson and Privates D. Haines, R. Flynn and E. Harris crept out of the camp. Unfortunately they failed to find their supply cache and in searching for it aroused the guards. They were all arrested and consigned to the wooden boxes. Conner was arrested, suggesting once again that the group had been betrayed although three of his helpers, Rifleman E. McAlonen, Private D. Tomlinson and Gunner S. Vickerson, remained undetected. However, the Chinese were up to their tricks and Conner was released on 30 June. Soon afterwards he attempted to escape, together with Corporal J. Calder, Lance Corporal W. Orr and Private H. Clarkson. But they were all arrested before they could leave the precincts of the camp.

And so began another Chinese hunt for evidence of the existence of an escape committee within the camp, but the brutal interrogation of the latest batch of escapers produced no positive results because it did not exist.

The last significant escape attempt of the season was made on 26 July by Rifleman C. Brierley and Private D. Richards. The party was to have included Fusilier Derek Kinne, but Kinne had ruptured himself weightlifting in order to get fit for the escape. When he heard they had gone he followed, despite having a double hernia. He was at liberty for two days but the other pair remained at liberty for a record period of ten days, which convinced the Chinese that they must have had outside help. They would never admit to weaknesses in their own security arrangements, believing as they did that escape without help was utterly impossible (which, indeed, was unfortunately very true).

No description of the mistreatment of p.o.w. in Korea would be complete without the story of Fusilier Derek Kinne of the Royal Northumberland Fusiliers, who, upon repatriation was awarded the George Cross for his gallantry and suffering. He was a 'K' volunteer who had joined up to avenge the death of his brother in battle. From the moment of capture he was a rebellious prisoner. He had made an escape attempt during the evacuation and upon arrival in Camp 1 he was continuously in trouble with the Chinese for ridiculing the compulsory indoctrination programme, threatening progressives and numerous other 'offences' and had been beaten up for striking back at a Chinese officer who had assaulted him. While confined to a storeroom for some offence the Chinese let him know that they believed he was plotting to escape with Richards and Brierley . He managed to slip out of his temporary prison to warn them, but they had already gone. He went after them and managed to travel eighteen miles with his injuries before he was recaptured. The Chinese were convinced that he could not have travelled so far with his injuries unless he'd had outside help and tortured him in their usual way by tying his hands behind his back, roping one leg to his hands and then throwing the rope over a beam and noosing it about his neck, leaving him balancing on one leg to avoid strangulation. After some hours he was quite literally at the end of his tether and agreed to give them the information that they demanded. He was taken to the camp HQ to start making a written report on his escape, prevaricating for three days on various excuses before seriously putting pen to paper. He produced eighteen pages which he refused to allow the Chinese to read until he had completed them. He had written a story entitled 'Goldilocks and the Three Bears' in which he had lampooned the Communist system and its supposed merits over capitalism which he confessed he much preferred. The Chinese were furious and lost their tempers, beating him until they had no more energy to beat him any more. They flung him into solitary confinement, periodically beating him with planks and finally handcuffed him and consigned him to the wooden boxes. One day he complained about the food he was receiving in the kennels and a particularly mean guard opened the door, fitted him with a fourth pair of handcuffs and ordered him to stand to attention, which was, of course, impossible inside the box. After being tormented for seven hours, Kinne refused to do as the guard ordered. He was hauled out of the hutch and beaten up. The guard commander arrived to join in the beating and struck Kinne a vicious blow with the butt of his sub-machine gun. The gun went off and killed its owner.

For the next five days Kinne was the victim of the Chinese revenge. They accused him of murder, stripped him of his clothes and beat him senseless repeatedly until they tired of punishing him. On 16 October he was tried before a military court for escaping and was sentenced to twelve months' imprisonment. When he complained that he'd been denied medical attention for his hernia the sentence was increased to eighteen months. He was transferred to the penal camp at Song-Ni to serve his sentence where he was again in trouble with his captors.

Brierley and Richards were also brutally treated in the effort to discover the existence of an organization helping escapers, but their interrogators again drew a blank. Richards was condemned to the wooden boxes for two and a half months and then sentenced to fifty-three days in a Korean jail and another five months in the camp's hard labour unit. Brierley was interrogated for forty days in the camp HQ before being sentenced to three months' hard labour.

The interrogation of all these escapers was long and agonizing and varied according to the demeanour of the individual. The patently stubborn and uninformative received the worst treatment and those who pretended to be co-operative were savagely beaten when their pretences were discovered. All of them were manhandled and physically maltreated and there was nothing in their treatment that could remotely be described as psychological. Many of them were repeatedly made to stand for days in the heat until they collapsed. Some were tightly bound with wire until they lost all feeling in their hands and arms and upon release experienced the excruciating agony of pins and needles as their circulation was restored. Many of them were subjected to the Chinese favourite form of torture, forcing their arms up their backs with the running end of the rope noosed about their necks. Nearly all of them were consigned to the wooden boxes, unable to stretch out, half-starved and foul from their own natural functions. Yet still they held out until tricked into confessing, though the written confessions were usually unsatisfactory and were obtained only after weeks of arguing and wrangling with their confessors about their contents.

At the beginning of August many of the escapers and their helpers who refused to provide adequate confessions were arraigned before a military tribunal in the cinema at Chongsong and after conviction were transferred to the penal camp at Song-Ni which ultimately contained about one hundred and thirty British and Americans. They were all consigned to the 'hole' along with a group of American reactionaries who had been caught assaulting leading progressives. Beyond the 'hole' the camp was surrounded by high fencing, armed patrols and machine guns and no pretence of Leniency. Five days later twenty three more reactionaries, including most of the remaining members of escape groups and their helpers, were quietly arrested and dispatched to Song-Ni. The inmates at this camp were fed with little food to deprive them of energy and were led to believe that should an armistice be signed before they had completed their sentences they would be detained until their sentences had been completed because they were convicted 'war criminals' outside the benefits of the Lenient Policy.

Upjohn remained at Chongsong to await a show trial. Soon afterwards all the sergeants were removed from their compound and sent to a camp exclusively for sergeants at Kuuptong, where there was a conventional non-political regime.

Thereafter there were few active reactionaries left in Chongsong where compulsory political indoctrination suddenly gave way to voluntary study groups similar to those that had evolved at Pyoktong, where it flourished. But events at Chongsong during the season had aroused widespread hatred against the progressives, all of whom were now indiscriminately branded as traitors by their fellow prisoners. One or two were savagely beaten up and all were promised further punishment upon repatriation, which seemed imminent in view of the progress being made at the Peace Talks. Amidst mounting tension Smee and two others who had played prominent parts in the annihilation of escapers and reactionaries were suddenly transferred to Pyoktong for their own safety. There, in the compound for progressives, Smee was made the secretary of the so-called Central Peace Committee as a reward for his services and his two companions were made committee members. They continued their propaganda activities with greater zest than had been prudent hitherto, safe from the wrath of those whom they had betrayed.

The final act in the offensive against reactionaries at Chongsong was

Upjohn's show trial which was held in the cinema where the Chinese set up an imposing military tribunal. The auditorium was packed with enemy officers, armed guards and delegations of prisoners imported from other camps to witness the proceedings and to assimilate its lessons. Upjohn and one or two of his helpers were brought before the tribunal and formally charged, but were not allowed to say anything in their own defence. The principal evidence was their own humiliating confessions, which they had to read to the tribunal. They were then sentenced by the President, reading from a prepared typescript. They were awarded a year's imprisonment in the 'hole' at Song-Ni.

After the sentence had been passed many of the prisoners in the audience were forced to sign statements to the effect that the 'trial' had been 'fair and just'. One of them, Lance Corporal C. McLaughlin, refused and was threatened with a loaded revolver, whereupon he printed his name.

From this point on life at Chongsong became conventional. The Peace Committee had been destroyed by the arrest or transfer of all its members. Smee and his two associates were now at Pyoktong. Upjohn, the Chairman of the camp's Daily Life Committee, his associates and Judas were transferred to Song-Ni. There was a rapid decline in political activity and by the end of December 1952 the Chinese were hotly denying that there had ever been any compulsory indoctrination and were taking considerable pains to search out and destroy the evidence, the notes and notebooks which the prisoners had earlier been forced to keep during lectures and discussion. However, some of the prisoners hid their notebooks and smuggled them out of captivity.

When, in January 1953, another analysis was made by A.I.9 of the extent of political collaboration among the ORs in Chongsong, it was found that it had increased a mere one per cent over the previous year and it remained at six per cent for the rest of the war.

This almost total failure of the enemy's indoctrination programme was very largely due to the spontaneous and widespread reactionary activities of the ORs. In attacking them with unmitigated brutality the Chinese destroyed all their pretences of Leniency and also revealed their reliance upon their foul informer system that riddled every squad, platoon and company of prisoners.

From the summer of 1952 to the summer of 1953 the prisoners led a fairly mundane existence, angry and frustrated by the interminable arguments between the belligerents at the Peace negotiations that delayed their repatriation for a year.

105

THE CARNE-BROWN 'PLOT'

(Camp 2 (Branch 1): Officers)

The Lenient Policy applied as much to officer-prisoners as it did to other ranks and the Chinese did not at first make any allowances for differences of education, social mores or traditions. All prisoners were regarded as of equal status and of the same low level of political consciousness – in the Communist interpretation of that term – and were subjected to the same programme of political indoctrination.

The American authorities freely admitted, after the war, that many of their officers had become progressives and had co-operated fairly freely with the enemy in running their domestic affairs and in the production of propaganda. Some of them, indeed, had been 'converted' to Communism and had refused repatriation at the end of the war.

It was these very facts that sparked an uproar in the British press when the Blue Book was published, revealing that only British Other Ranks had become progressives and that no British officer had participated in the production of enemy propaganda. Our military authorities were immediately suspected of a cover-up and, despite many provocative accusations and jibes in the Press, there was no official response, which simply compounded their suspicions.

It would be foolish to suppose that the continuous presentation of one-sided propaganda had no effect whatsoever upon the British officers' opinions and attitudes. Their status gave them no special immunity. In fact it did raise doubts in the minds of many of the officers over a number of issues like the causes of the war, the legality of the American and British intervention and above all over the question of whether or not the U.S. Air Force had dropped germ-bombs on North Korea. But such doubts did not seem to them to justify disloyalty and were counterbalanced by their own very recent experiences of Chinese Leniency and its unscrupulous, dishonest, deceitful and inhuman nature.

With the exception of the Turks, who executed the only one of their number who co-operated with their captors and whose language and culture pattern prevented the Chinese from coming to grips with them, the British officers were the only group against whom the Chinese policy may be said to have failed completely. This is not because they were supermen or heroes. They very quickly learned that overt displays of courage and intransigence played directly into the hands of their captors who were only too happy to consign the culprits to cold, damp dungeons. Imprisoned reactionaries were not much use if they were unable to perpetrate acts of resistance or organize others to do likewise. So what was it about the officers that enabled them to resist the full effects of the Lenient Policy?

As far as enemy propaganda was concerned it was their education, but, as we have seen in the previous chapters, the Chinese could only make their propaganda stick and enforce co-operation in political activities by smashing the existing military organization and its chain of command and by removing any individual or group that offered any resistance.

The command hierarchy among the ORs in the two main camps comprised only three ranks, those of corporal, lance corporal and private, and by their very numbers gave no clear precedence to individuals holding a particular rank over the many others of identical rank. Consequently there was no clear chain of command, a situation foreseen in the Geneva Convention which placed authority in their elected representatives. The officers, however, possessed a clear hierarchical range of five distinct ranks, from Lieutenant Colonel to Second Lieutenant, with a traditional system of seniorities within each rank which placed every officer in a precise position in relation to the others of identical rank within the total hierarchy. Moreover, the position of every individual officer was known to all the other officers. There was, therefore, a clear chain of command acknowledged by every officer. Consequently if any of them was imprisoned for exercising his authority, his role could be assumed by the next one in the hierarchy. As has already been said, there was no such system among the American officers who were additionally blighted by inter-service rivalry.

But the maintenance of the chain of command was not the principal reason for the failure of the Lenient Policy on the British officers. Of far greater importance was their social mores, already noted in a previous chapter and summarized aptly in Derek Kinne's remarks about 'their fancy ways' giving them something special. As already mentioned, at the moment of capture Colonel Carne had let it be known what sort of conduct he expected of his officers in captivity and they were anxious to live up to it. The importance of these social forces within the British officer group cannot be over-stressed since they provided social cohesion and a code of conduct to guide the behaviour of every individual. There was little quibbling over who should do what under this or that set of circumstances because Army regulations or tradition or social conventions catered for almost every kind of situation.

The almost total collapse of morale and discipline among the American prisoners was due in no small part to the absence of any parallel system among them. As the U.S. Army authorities freely admitted, their men were also culturally pre-disposed to behaving in their own selfish interests, even if this was at the expense of their fellows. One U.S. study said that thirty-three per cent of them showed little or no concern for their compatriots and only thirteen per cent showed strong concern. This left just over half who showed only mild concern, evidently not enough to sustain discipline and morale. Moreover, their culture pattern preached equality of status and did not make such marked distinctions between officers and enlisted men, all of whom had been brought up to accept opportunistic behaviour in a highly competitive environment. It is not surprising, therefore, that, in adversity, these characteristics were enhanced and led to the exploitation of the helpless which was so destructive of morale and discipline.

The slight improvement in living conditions resulting from the Chinese takeover of the Yalu River camps in April 1951 produced a partial restoration of American morale. But it was the example set by the British officers in both Camps 1 and 5 that stimulated attempts by American officers to restore discipline and their chain of command. However, the Americans were frustrated in the latter by their lack of any inter-service system of determining seniority, so that inter-service rivalry prevented a single chain. The result was that they usually had three spokesmen, one for each of their Services, whereas the British had but one.

In Camp 5 there were only five British officers and the Chinese dealt with them as a potential source of resistance by scattering them individually among different American platoons.

The Chinese absolutely refused to accept any system of command and control based upon rank, ostensibly on the grounds that it was 'un-democratic'. But their real reason was that they saw it as a mechanism for maintaining the cohesion and discipline of the rankers as well as the officer-group and a threat to their plans to impose their own Communist social structure and its system of controlling the behaviour of individuals.

Even before the second column of British p.o.w. including Colonel Carne, arrived in Camp 1, Major 'Sam' Weller, the SBO, had been removed from the ORs compound for exercising his authority. With the arrival of the second column, Colonel Carne became the SBO. He was under no illusions about what would happen to him if he was caught giving orders because he and his second-in-command, Denis Harding, had already been strung up by their wrists during the evacuation. Nevertheless in his unassuming manner he succeeded for some time in taking command. The Chinese failure to catch him red-handed only increased their determination to catch him out on some other account. He was placed under close surveillance by the Chinese staff and presumably also by their informers.

As with the ORs in Camp 1 the officers were ordered to elect a Daily Life Committee soon after their arrival. They were treated to a lengthy explanation of the 'correct' and 'democratic' methods of selection. As usual the Chinese maintained their 'right' to vet the candidates and ratify all appointments, conditions which the officers refused to accept. Long and futile arguments followed and the Chinese began to lose patience. They applied gentle pressure by re-squadding many of the officers, placing them in American platoons and putting the more stubborn of them in a reactionary squad. This and a few other prods persuaded the officers to nominate a committee acceptable to the Chinese, though it ostentatiously failed to meet or to exercise its authority. The domestic affairs of the camp continued to be managed in a fashion which the Chinese regarded as highly irregular.

At about the same time two Anglo-American half-companies of officers and sergeants were paraded to hear the news that they could write letters home, providing they included accounts of the good treatment they were receiving from the Chinese People's Volunteers. The Chinese invited prisoners who did not wish to avail themselves of this wonderful opportunity to fall out and, to their utter astonishment, all but one of the assembled prisoners, an American officer, fell out! For this ingratitude they were all put on fatigues, carrying one hundredweight sacks of rice. Next day the Chinese climbed down, excusing themselves by saying that the prisoners had misunderstood the previous day's instructions. As a sop, they invited the prisoners to write home without conditions. But they now had further proof of an organized conspiracy.

Early in July the Chinese ordered every p.o.w. company to produce a representative to help draft a telegram of greeting to the Communist-organized Chicago Peace Conference. The British refused to participate, so the Chinese found an American to draft and sign a petition on their behalf.

When, in August, the Chinese began to take soundings in the ORs' compounds about creating a Peace Committee they must have realized the sort of reception they would get in the officers' compounds. They pre-empted organized resistance by quietly arresting Colonel Carne and transferring him to Camp 5 at Pyoktong, where, they hoped, he would have little influence among the predominantly progressive population. Simultaneously Major Weller, a constant thorn in their sides, and Captain W.L. Morris were both arrested on the excuse that they had falsified their autobiographies, which indeed they had. Hoping to use them to apply timely pressure on the British officer-group, the pair were given a sound beating and were then paraded before their colleagues to hear them abused and threatened by D.P. Wong, who had been transferred from Pyoktong to help the local staff deal with the officers' resistance. In the most offensive terms the victims were reminded of their 'war guilt' and the punishment awaiting unmitigated 'war criminals', i.e. death.

It was upon this threatening note that the Peace Campaign was launched with orders to elect company and camp Peace Committees. Evidently the Chinese had second thoughts about allowing the officers to participate. They were prohibited from voting as punishment for their past 'crimes' and for refusing to take part in the Peace Parade scheduled for 1 October. To stop them interfering, all the British and American officers, about 350 of them, were transferred to a new camp specially created for them at Pin Chon-Ni, ten miles east of Pyoktong and four miles south of the Yalu River. Surrounded by wire, and guarded, the camp was centred upon a schoolhouse and its outbuildings. The Camp Commandant was the fanatical Ding Fang, with the brutal D.P Wong as his chief interpreter. His staff of seventeen officers were terrified of him. There were five members of the Chinese staff in addition to D.P Wong with whom the British p.o.w. had close contact. In charge of security was Chen Chung Hwei, a little hunch-back with big darting eyes who spent a lot of his time creeping about the camp spying on the inmates. A dangerous interrogator was Big Chu, five feet ten inches tall and with an excellent command of English. Dealing with mail and discipline was his namesake Little Chu, a jack of all trades, short-sighted and frog-eyed. In charge of the failing political study programme was Sun, a propagandist whose grasp of his subject was tenuous and who read his lectures from his notes. Lastly there was the polite Nui, who looked like an unctuous clergyman, except that although he was invariably polite he was an inveterate liar. He was responsible for the camp entertainment and recreation.

The immediate effect of the transfer to the new camp was to put the Americans in the majority, and an American officer was needed to became the Senior United Nations Officer (SUNO). Not unnaturally the Americans disliked the idea of their interests being represented by a British minority group but once again they could not agree among themselves as to who was to be their senior officer. Eventually they agreed to the election of a panel of three, one from each of their Services, which would be joined by a British representative to act in secret on behalf of all the officers.

Colonel Carne was the SBO, but he was being closely watched by both the Chinese and informers and he had been left in no doubt what would happen to him if he was caught exercising his authority. Consequently, his deputy, Major Denis Harding, acted as a cut-out and became the British representative to relay Colonel Carne's advice.

As usual, soon after reaching their new camp the officers were ordered to elect their Daily Life Committee 'democratically'. By this time they realized that there would be no use arguing with the Chinese and instead the elections were quietly engineered so that the senior USAF officer, Lieutenant Colonel G. Brown, was 'unanimously' elected President and Major Denis Harding became the Vice-President. The other members were likewise elected with suspicious unanimity. The Chinese were well aware that the elections had been rigged; their informers had told them. But they accepted the situation for the time being while they sought further evidence of a 'conspiracy' and the identity of the chief conspirators. It was not long in coming.

The catering member of the Daily Life Committee was caught red-handed passing food and clothing to imprisoned reactionaries. Also, the political studies sub-committee resigned en bloc as a protest at the political bias of the compulsory study programme. But the issue which really riled the Chinese and sparked revenge was the prisoners' refusal to send a Christmas message of greeting to General Peng-Teh-Huei, the C in C of the People's Volunteers. When serious reprisals were threatened, the secret panel issued orders for the prisoners to comply by wishing the C in C "an early peace and a speedy return to China!" It took some time for the enemy to understand the subtle implications of this greeting.

It was too much to hope that the existence of the secret panel and the identities of its members would remain secret for very long. Not only were the Chinese kept informed by their informers but they received confirmation of their suspicions when a very naïve young Marine Corps officer informed his interrogator that he could not answer his questions unless he was given permission to do so by Colonel Brown, the head of the panel.

On 11 January 1952 the three American members of the panel were arrested. Since they had failed to provide themselves with a cover story their contradictory statements provided the Chinese with further clues that led to the arrest of Denis Harding on 23 January and Colonel Carne on the 26th. Another American Air Force officer, Major D. McGhee, who had organized the resignation of the study sub-committee, was also arrested on suspicion of being one of the leading 'plotters'. All of them were charged with conspiring to set up a resistance organization, plotting against the camp authorities and various other charges which according to the Chinese disciplinary code, carried the maximum penalties of death or imprisonment for life. During their interrogation the Chinese dropped all pretence of leniency. They were spared no indignity. They were beaten, starved, deprived of sleep and necessities, exposed to extremes of heat in boiler houses and stood out in the freezing cold of the Korean winter, as well as being tortured.

On 8 February they were paraded before the entire camp to make their 'confessions' with the obvious intention of discrediting them before their subordinates. Colonel Carne and Denis Harding simply admitted to breaking unspecified Chinese' regulations. After a fatuous pretence of legality the Chinese passed sentences. Colonel Carne, Colonel Brown, Major Harding and presumably all the others were sentenced to six months' solitary confinement. The sentences meant nothing; Colonel Carne was kept in solitary confinement in a remote hut for eighteen months. Harding was isolated for fifteen months in a cowshed.

The Chinese utterly failed to stigmatize any of the 'culprits' of this so-called 'Carne-Brown Plot'. None of the British or American officers were under any illusions about how the confessions had been obtained or the monstrously unjust penalties for their so-called 'crimes'. Harding in particular displayed all the symptoms of his torture in his useless dangling wrists. The Chinese themselves evidently had misgivings over the staging of the 'trial' and intercepted several British officers on their way out of the 'court' to ask them what sort of impression it had made upon their fellow prisoners.

Once isolated, Colonel Carne was subjected to relentless daily interrogation, the objective of which seems to have been to force him into composing a series of documents that would make him appear to be their most prestigious leading progressive in their propaganda campaign. Daily he was compelled to write essays on the usual political issues, in the hope of harrying him into condemning the Americans and the United Nations for their aggression, into pleading for peace on Communist terms, etc. They kept at him day and night until they had worn him out. When, eventually, after months of harrying and writing they thought they had succeeded in getting him to produce a statement to their liking and rushed across the room to collect it Colonel Carne screwed up the rice paper and swallowed it!

Between the endless days of interrogations and writing Colonel Carne took to sculpting miniature objects out of volcanic rocks picked up outside his hut. His tools were a chisel made from a piece of metal from the instep of an American army boot sharpened on the granite doorstep of his hut, a rock as a hammer and the granite doorstep of his hut to smooth the surfaces of his pieces. On repatriation he managed to bring three of his sculptures with him, one of his regimental badge, one of a bullock in a field and one of a cross, which he donated to Gloucester Cathedral.

The Chinese had, of course, discovered that the Daily Life Committee had been used as a cover for the 'Carne-Brown Plot' and therefore disbanded it, ordering the prisoners to elect a new one by the 'proper democratic process'. The prisoners refused to do so unless their captors recognized the authority of the senior British and American officers to run their domestic affairs free from political and other interference. The Chinese refused to accept these conditions and in retaliation arrested several of the officers who had disseminated the orders of the secret panel.

In the face of these pressures the prisoners agreed among themselves to concede to the Chinese orders, but would again rig the elections to make Major Ryan, who was now the SBO, the new President of the Daily Life Committee. The other committee appointments were similarly pre-arranged. The Chinese refused to accept Ryan's election. In his stead they appointed as President the 'broken' former SUNO from Camp 5, now a willing collaborator, a move which the prisoners trumped by refusing to elect anybody to serve under him.

Once again the Chinese were forced to retreat and accept what for them must have been a humiliating defeat and loss of face to add to their failure to obtain any results with their compulsory political study programme. Ever since the officers had been moved to Pin Chon-Ni there had been a steady reduction in the number of lectures and compulsory study periods and they fizzled out altogether in March 1952, supposedly to allow the prisoners time to clean their quarters after the winter. The spring cleaning dragged on for three months before there was any more propaganda. But when it came, it was probably more effective than anything the Chinese had concocted previously.

To this day there has never been a satisfactory explanation of the reasons why the Communists accused the United Nations, or, more specifically, the Americans, of waging germ warfare on North Korea. In special interrogation centres something like ninety-one very unfortunate United States Air Force and Marines aircrewmen and one Royal Canadian Air Force officer, Squadron Leader A. MacKenzie, were subjected to prolonged and horrific interrogations to force them to confess to waging germ warfare.

Inside all the p.o.w. camps in Korea the Chinese mounted a special campaign to convince their captives of America's most dastardly 'war crime'. Selected groups of British and American prisoners, including the officers, were compelled to study the 'evidence' which included the reports of allegedly politically unbiased commissions of international lawyers and scientists and the particularly damning confessions of two USAF lieutenants, Enoch and Quinn. The p.o.w. were also compelled to visit a photographic exhibition which had been specially set up to furnish 'irrefutable proof' of this latest of America's 'war crimes'. This included photos of Korean civilians in face masks decontaminating their villages, pictures of the germ bombs, suspiciously undamaged after being dropped from a great height and also photos of the American aircrew prisoners said to have been responsible.

The 'germ warfare' propaganda is known to have been more effective in convincing the British officers of its 'truth' than all the rest of the enemy propaganda and compulsory indoctrination put together. They possessed little knowledge of bacteriological warfare and the horrific consequences that would have resulted from the unleashing of just small amounts. Consequently they were unable to detect the obvious symptoms of a hoax. Suspicions were aroused in the minds of nearly all of them as to whether the Americans had dropped a few experimental bombs. Despite the prisoners' doubts it does not seem to have produced any additional souring of Anglo-American relations in the officers' camp.

In Pin Chon-Ni there were no more compulsory lectures or study and subsequently there were no voluntary study groups as there had been at Pyoktong and Chongsong. The total failure of the Lenient Policy spurred the Chinese efforts to crush resistance and reactionary activities within the camp. Beginning soon after Easter, there were numerous attacks upon the officers' leaders in search of real and imaginary 'plots'.

114

In May Major Ryan disappeared and his colleagues never saw him again until he was repatriated in September 1953. He had in fact been removed for interrogation by a visiting team of North Koreans, including the infamous Major Pak, in search of belated military information. Ryan took the opportunity to accuse his North Korean tormentors of murdering two of his sergeants, Sergeants Kavanagh and Nugent. For his impudence he was flung into a rat-infested, filthy outhouse for two months and subsequently transferred to the officers' penal camp at Chang-Ni. There he was compelled to perform unsavoury fatigues until November when he was arrested on a trumped-up charge of attempted murder because the door of his ramshackle quarters had collapsed upon his sentry. For three months he was continuously ill-treated by his interrogators to no avail. Finally he was sentenced to a face-saving month of solitary confinement.

As early as April 1952 the Chinese had sought an excuse for convicting Major 'Sam' Weller of serious offences. He had made himself a thorough nuisance to the Chinese from the moment of his capture and had served several spells in jails. During April 1953, however, the Chinese sent the American president of the non-existent Daily Life Committee to sound out his views on how the domestic affairs of the camp could be arranged in the present stand-off situation. Weller informed him bluntly that the British officers would refuse to co-operate with a Chinese-nominated committee, except over matters of sanitation, health and welfare. The conversation was, of course, relayed directly to the Chinese and a month later Weller was called to the Chinese camp HQ. Again he was asked his views on the way the domestic affairs of the camp might be run and almost before he could answer he was accused of inciting the British officers to resist the camp authorities. A heated argument ensued and, in an attempt to bring Weller to heel, Colonel Carne was brought out of his solitary confinement to confront Weller with the intention of getting the Colonel to order him to co-operate. Colonel Carne gave his orders in a master-piece of double-talk which sailed over the heads of the Chinese. They were evidently satisfied. So was Weller, who conveyed the Colonel's wishes to his brother officers.

In the middle of July and on 1 August the British p.o.w. organized spontaneous demonstrations of their loyalty to their new Queen, including the singing of the National Anthem. The Chinese were furious at the outburst of 'patriotic songs' as they called our National Anthem. Weller was arrested and accused of being responsible and after a heated argument he was released. Two days later he was re-arrested, bound tightly with wire, slapped in the face and accused of a long list of serious 'crimes'. They included organizing demonstrations, conspiring to escape and organizing an escape committee among the ORs at Chongsong before he left. According to the Chinese disciplinary code, these 'crimes' carried the maximum penalty of death or imprisonment for life. Of course the p.o.w. had no means of knowing if their captors were bluffing and were all too well aware that the Communists were quite capable of retaining them in captivity to complete their sentences after the signing of any Armistice.

Thus did another SBO disappear from the compound. After prolonged interrogation during which he was forced to stand to attention for periods of six, twelve and twenty four hours, mostly in the pitiless heat, he was sentenced to a year's imprisonment on 21 July, seven days before the Armistice was signed. He was one of the very last prisoners to be repatriated, causing great anxiety that he would in fact be detained to complete his sentence.

The prisoners appointed another SBO to take his place and when he was arrested his place was assumed by another officer and so on until a succession of Captains became the SBO.

The story of 'reactionary' activities in Pin Chon-Ni would not be complete without mentioning escape activities. Professionally the British officers were far better equipped than the ORs to gauge their chances of escaping across the terrain of North Korea. And they had the very distinct advantage of their close-knit society for containing their secrets and reducing the chances of them falling to the ears of informers. However, although seven officers, five warrant officers, three Australian pilots and two South African pilots attempted to escape, they had no greater success than the ORs. Altogether forty-one British and American prisoners attempted to escape during the 1952 season. Several of the escape parties were betrayed by informers.

The Chinese were ceaselessly on the alert for an escape committee of the World War II type, but no such organization existed among the British p.o.w. Even if it had, it would have had little opportunity to function because of the continuous arrest and imprisonment of officers for various infractions and the continuous attempts to smash their chain of command. The Chinese pounced upon all escapers or suspected escapers and suspected helpers, regardless of whether they were associated with the current attempt, and usually jailed them on trumped-up charges. It is unlikely that any co-ordinated centralized escape committee could have thrived in such an environment. The Carne-Brown 'plot' had taught everybody the dangers of any kind of co-ordinated action and the British officers had numerous examples of betrayals by American informers.

Therefore, search as they did, Ding Fang and his gang of thugs could never discover an 'official' British escape committee of the World War II type because it simply did not exist.

However, in January 1953 the interrogators did unearth an informal so-called escape committee in the officers' penal camp at Chang-Ni. It comprised a small group, mostly of Americans, but included Flying Officer M.O.Berg, a South African serving in the RAF. Berg was betrayed. No doubt with the RAF's escaping history in Germany well in mind, the Chinese pounced on him and transferred him to Pin Chon-Ni where Ding Fang's team pounded him with questions for about four months, threatening him with twenty years' imprisonment for being the leader of the 'plot'. Driven almost to the end of his tether, Berg refused to betray his colleagues and was eventually released into the officers' compound.

The Chinese were chasing a myth. If the British officers or warrant officers wished to organize an escape, individuals made their own arrangements, kept their intentions to themselves and took off at a suitable opportunity. And because of the tailing-off of compulsory political activities after the transfer to Pin Chon-Ni escape activity was less disruptive in its effects upon the Lenient Policy than it had been among the ORs in Chongsong.

10

INDOCTRINATION, PROPAGANDA & 'BRAINWASHING'

According to fiction and the speculations of journalists and certain publicity-seeking psychiatrists, Indoctrination and Interrogation are two aspects of a technique which has been widely portrayed as a scientifically-based process invented by the Russians and variously described as 'Menticide' by psychiatrists and as 'Brainwashing' by journalists.

The term 'Brainwashing' did not make its first appearance in the English vocabulary until 1954, that is, after the conclusion of the Korean War, when it became attached to the Chinese (*not* Russian) treatment of a relatively small number of *American* p.o.w. who had been forced to confess to having waged bacteriological warfare on North Korea. The term was coined by an American journalist, Edward Hunter, in his book about the Chinese Communists system of educating and re-educating the Chinese masses. It's title was *Brainwashing in Red China* and in it he made a distinction, which he later retracted when he discovered the journalistic mileage to be obtained from his concepts, between 'Brainwashing' and 'Brain-changing'. He wrote, "Brainwashing is indoctrination, a relatively simple procedure. Brain-changing is immeasurably more sinister and complicated".

This is not the place for speculation on the theoretical possibilities of what Hunter originally described as 'Brain-changing' and what journalists and the public now think of as 'Brainwashing'. To attempt to do so would involve a very complicated psychological dissertation of numerous theories of human cognition and their hierarchical structures, all of which would be open to challenge by experts on cognition. In any case it would all remain in the realm of theoretical speculation since, for humanitarian reasons, there would be no possibility of substantiating the validity of any of the theories or even indicating which of them is the most plausible in the light of hard evidence.

But of greater relevance is that such speculation would be entirely inappropriate to this history since *none of the British p.o.w.* was subjected to psychologically significant techniques. As we have seen in the previous chapters, there was nothing subtle or of particular psychological significance in the manner in which the British p.o.w. were indoctrinated and subjected to propaganda warfare. It was an assault upon their opinions and attitudes. Opinions and attitudes rank low in the hierarchy of cognition and are therefore superficial. By no stretch of the imagination can their alteration or modification qualify as 'Brain-changing' (i.e. structural alterations to the cognitive processes) as originally envisaged by Hunter or 'Brainwashing' as envisaged by the popular press. The prisoners' confessions of their so-called 'crimes' were extracted from them by brutal physical assaults upon their persons and in no way did the substance of their confessions reflect their true feelings. Consequently talk about 'Brainwashing' really is inappropriate.

The subject of Attitudes and Attitude Change is one that has received an enormous amount of attention and research from professional psychologist, all of it inconclusive. Little of it is helpful in analysing the Chinese techniques. A more pragmatic approach is needed, although some reference to technical aspects of cognition (thought processes) is unavoidable. However, our attention should be focused upon the North Korean/Russian and Chinese propaganda programmes, their substance, the manner and means by which they were carried into effect, and their measurable effects.

When the news reached London that the prisoners were being subjected to intensive indoctrination the immediate reaction of the military staff was to regard it as a back-door method of interrogation. It was argued that the purpose of this type of attack upon the prisoners' attitudes was to get them to give away military information. What other reason could there be for political propaganda? There was, of course, an element of truth in this but events soon revealed that the majority of the British p.o.w. who were being successfully indoctrinated were those of the lowest ranks who had the least access to any significant tactical or strategic information. Hence, as an interrogation technique, indoctrination was a very inefficient and long-winded method, with a very poor return for effort, though doubtless it did yield some grains of information of military value.

Only in retrospect was it seen to have considerable value to the Chinese system of security controls. And, as we have seen, the identification of prisoners as potential progressives or reactionaries was fundamental to both the indoctrination and security programmes of the Chinese.

The North Korean indoctrination programme and the difficulties they encountered with American and British p.o.w. have been explained in some detail in Chapter 4. It was short lived and its students, educated and well trained in the Russian version of Communism and its concepts and procedures, were contemptuously subdued by the Chinese when the Peace Fighters arrived in Camp 5. However, it did reveal that the indoctrinators overestimated the political interests and awareness and the literary capacities of the British p.o.w., whereas the Chinese went to the other extreme.

We now know from the interrogation of Chinese soldiers captured by U.N. forces that the entire indoctrination programme inflicted upon British and other U.N. prisoners of war was identical in principle and practice to that inflicted by the Communists upon their own soldiers in the early stages of their military training. It was characterized by the same system of lecturing, followed up with small study groups and harrying by platoon political officers.

In Korea the successful indoctrination of British and all other occidentals was severely handicapped by two very important characteristics of oriental thinking. As the report on the Kanggye experiment revealed, a senior Chinese Political officer early recognized fundamental differences between their former oriental p.o.w. and the newly captured occidentals, and he wrote of "our insufficient knowledge about their character and ways of thinking". What he described as "ways of thinking" would today be classed as a "cognitive style", and what he ascribed to ignorance of their "character" was probably the huge cultural divide between their culture pattern and those of Western societies, something which the Chinese at first failed or refused to recognize.

The hallmark of the traditional Chinese cognitive style is that it is "situation oriented", i.e. appropriate behavioural responses are assumed to be implicit in the existing situation; put in another way, the individual is expected to think and behave according to the hints radiated by the prevailing situation. Furthermore the Chinese structure their ideas, (what we call reasoning) according to traditional rules of inter-personal relations and with due deference to age and status, i.e. by social factors, not by what we would call the rules of logic. The Western style is not implicit. It is explicit. If we want somebody to do something we tell them what to do, which is regarded as bad manners in Chinese society. And we have speci-

120

fied formulae for structuring ideas and concepts. These differences can be illustrated in the following example. The Chinese would repeatedly tell a prisoner that he had been arrested for breaking the rules and when he asked, "what rules?" they would reply "You know what you have been doing", leaving the prisoner to guess what infraction they wanted him to admit to. The same device was applied to written material. The unfortunate prisoner would not be told specifically what he was to incorporate in his political essay or confession. He would be compelled to write reams only to have his efforts torn up and ordered to try again and again until he guessed what might meet with their approval.

The implicit cognitive style of the Chinese has been seen by some writers as primary evidence of an insidious Communist scientific psychological technique of 'Brainwashing' (i.e. 'Brain-changing'), by suggestion, whereas in fact it is a very ancient Chinese educational tradition and is not something invented in this century by the Communists. In any case, if and when a prisoner was brought to pen a satisfactory statement or confession by such methods, it does not follow that he sincerely believed what he had written. In most cases of this kind among the p.o.w. in Korea, belief was absent; all utterances had been made under duress. Witness the methods used upon the Peace Fighters of Pyongyang and upon those involved with the Peace campaigns in Camps 1 and 5. Only a handful believed what they had written.

The second important difference, the Chinese culture bias, was very evident from what they expected the prisoners to write in their autobiographies. Their first Western prisoners were regarded as peasant conscripts, because, prior to Korea, almost all common soldiers captured by the Communists during the civil war in China had been uneducated peasants. The Chinese insisted that because British ORs were common soldiers they were uneducated peasants who had been duped into fighting by wicked capitalist imperialist propaganda. British p.o.w. were angrily rebuked for claiming to own houses, cars, motor bikes and other property, but no chickens or pigs. And any ranker claiming to have received a higher education was immediately suspected of being a spy or an officer posing as a ranker. All educated Chinese were regarded as 'Unreliables' by the Communists.

It is not known for certain how long it took the senior Chinese political officers to realize their mistakes, but it must have been many months after the start of the compulsory indoctrination programme. One can imagine the dogmatic senior political officers refusing to accept the feedback they were getting from their younger interpreters who were in direct contact with the p.o.w. and had more recent knowledge of Western culture because they had obtained their language skills in Hong Kong or Malaya or in Western mission educational institutions.

In addition to their alien cognitive style and the manner in which the Chinese reasoned, their thinking was additionally infested with Marxist economic and social notions, notions that belonged to the previous century. According to the autocratic Communist indoctrinators, their precepts were "self-evident to any right-minded person" and consequently only the insane or the criminally inclined would dare to question their validity. They expected, indeed demanded, that their 'students' accepted their authoritative assertions on trust, and woe betide the individual who challenged them. He would be told not to be 'smart'. Being 'smart' was regarded as a classic symptom of reactionary thinking.

The cultural differences between East and West were, and still are, huge. There can be no better example of the differences than their attitudes towards compulsory public confessions. One of the main reasons why the Chinese Communists compelled people to make humiliating public confessions was because they were very well aware of the huge social stigma attached to such an act in traditional Chinese culture. For the victim it produced unbearable public humiliation, loss of face and the public destruction of his self-esteem. Traditionally it often led the victim to commit suicide. The staff of the p.o.w. camps never seem to have recognized that to Western eyes a public confession and expression of remorse, or even a public self-criticism by a prisoner, was regarded by other prisoners as an utterly alien performance, foreign to our culture and only made under duress. It was proof that the confessor had been tortured into manufacturing a statement of guilt. The very language of the confession was alien in concept and wording. It attracted no shame, only heartfelt sympathy for the victim. Occasionally some of the British prisoners dared to turn the performance into a pantomime or used it as a vehicle to convey important information by innuendo – something the Chinese had not bargained for. Rarely had they met prisoners who would dare to violate the solemnity of the occasion and risk savage reprisals, even execution. They were rarely able to interpret the innuendo. They were taken by surprise by the reactions of the audience, by the applause, boos or catcalls, which alerted their suspicions that the British prisoners' public confessions contained hidden messages (which indeed they did). But it did not stop the Chinese from continuing to extract them from the reactionaries.

Thus all the enemy propaganda was besmirched with these important and fundamental cognitive and cultural characteristics, alien behaviour recognizable by every single British prisoner, insurmountable handicaps to the acceptance of Communist assertions and a hindrance to the effective indoctrination of the majority. An additional impediment to the acceptance of the propaganda was that the p.o.w., unlike Chinese nationals over whom the Communists had a lifelong 'hold', were aware that they would return, sooner rather than later, to their own countries and cultures, so that there was no long-term lifesaving obligation upon them to absorb the propaganda and the Communist way of life. This was a very important disincentive.

In its earliest phases the compulsory indoctrination programme had two main prongs. The first was to undermine the prisoners' faiths in their own government and institutions and the second was the ceaseless highlighting of the supposed economic and social benefits of Communism and its alleged superiority over capitalism in all of its manifestations. It was Russia, the Communists asserted, that had won the war in the Far East and liberated Korea from the Japanese yoke; it was Russia that had kept to the letter of the agreement made with its wartime Allies at Potsdam and Yalta to make Korea a free and democratic country (in the Communist interpretation of the term 'democratic'). It was America that had sabotaged all negotiations for the unification of North and South and free elections – witness the Syngman Rhee telegrams (which were shown to selected individuals among the early progressives). America had responded to the withdrawal of Soviet troops (in fact stealthily replaced by Soviet-trained Korean troops) at the end of the war by setting up the puppet Syngman Rhee and his corrupt government which had held phoney elections under police supervision (which was indeed true). America had created the artificial division of Korea and had made a secret military pact with the gangster Syngman Rhee and encouraged him to make 1,314 raids across the border into North Korea.

The Achilles heel of the United Nations intervention was the rottenness of the Syngman Rhee regime which the January captives especially had witnessed with their own eyes. According to the Communists, 630,000 Koreans had been arrested as spies in Rhee's reign of terror and 150,000 men, women and children had been shot in the winter of 1950/51. The British troops were under no illusions about the nature of the South Korean regime and all must have wondered whether it was worth defending. And they must have wondered if it was worth risking their lives fighting over a devastated landscape to save a primitive oriental way of life. However, the experiences of the British prisoners at the hands of the North Koreans must have left them in no doubt that the Korean regimes, North or South of the 38th Parallel, were as bad as one another and the shrewder of them doubtless realized that they were not fighting exclusively for the benefit of the Koreans but against the much greater threat of global Communism.

The legality of the United Nations intervention was as controversial then as it has been many times since. It was an issue that taxed the brains of international lawyers world-wide and it was impossible for the common soldier to judge the legality for himself. He had to take his Government's viewpoint on trust and its viewpoint, like every other viewpoint, was open to challenge. The Communists lost no opportunity to take up the challenge and brand it as illegal.

America was portrayed as the arch-villain, a role which gained much credence when the British p.o.w. saw for themselves the unscrupulous behaviour of the American p.o.w. in Camps 1 and 5 when those camps were controlled by the North Koreans. Anti-American feeling among the British p.o.w., officers and other ranks, was rife and remained so throughout their captivity, except that the officers kept the degree of their feelings to themselves. The Communists rubbed salt into Anglo-American relations by telling the British p.o.w. that the British Government was ingratiating itself with America in order to obtain dollars to prop up its ramshackle economy. Every British p.o.w. must have been well aware of the tenuous position of the British economy in the immediate post-war years and its reliance on American aid and must have wondered if they had indeed been sent to war in Korea as part of an Anglo-American agreement for economic aid.

These and many other barbs of Communist propaganda might have been more wounding to more prisoners had the Chinese taken the trouble to map out a structured indoctrination programme and carried it out with informed and convincing speakers. But their senior political officers, hardened old campaigners though they were, could neither speak English nor had any up to date knowledge of the British way of life. Their arrogant beliefs in the infallibility of their own antiquated ideas of capitalist Britain were passed on to their younger, English-speaking subordinates as indisputable facts. These younger men, equally arrogant in their beliefs in the veracity of their knowledge of all things British, were additionally handicapped by their unfamiliarity with idiomatic English and by their very amateur teaching abilities. Their haphazard efforts lacked convincing substance, hopped between disparate topics and their delivery was not only tedious in the extreme but became a laughing stock to the British

124

p.o.w. who greeted their assertions with catcalls and boos, causing them huge loss of face and resulting in savage reprisals.

The Chinese never seemed to appreciate the most obvious flaw in their ceaseless declarations of the superiority of Communism over Capitalism. Every single prisoner must have asked himself why, if Communism was so superior, they were nearly starving, why they and their captors' standard of living was so obviously inferior to those of the Western nations, why they and the Chinese staff were without comparable medical attention, adequate food and civilized living accommodation. Instead they were all herded into Korean hovels devoid of elementary plumbing and sanitation and overrun by lice, bugs and other vermin.

When the Chinese assumed control of the camps and instituted their compulsory study programme there was a marginal improvement in the speakers' mastery of their topics but their programme was hopelessly disjointed and topics became increasingly tedious. "How to recognize the USSR" and "How to recognize the USA" from their foreign policies were hardly inspiring to serious study. Other topics included The History of the People's Liberation Army, Money and the Class Struggle, and The Democratic Reformation and the Democratic Structure of North Korea. Sometimes adjacent lectures possessed contradictory themes such as The Inevitability of War in the Imperialist Epoch, coupled on the same day with Peaceful Co-existence. Unfortunately for the prisoners there was no escaping this turgid stuff; the lectures were followed by compulsory small-group discussion, comparable to tutorials, with set questions demanding written answers whether or not the prisoners comprehended the substance of the talk. And failure to produce acceptable answers was, as we have seen, punished, primarily with the reduction or withdrawal of food.

The Chinese Political Officers were quite incapable of appreciating that the dreary essence of their lectures was in itself defeating and lacking in a modicum of interest to all but a few. But they persisted with their inflexible lecture programme of mass indoctrination for nine months out of a long tradition of 'educating' the Chinese masses in such topics. It had worked on the Chinese peasants for a quarter of a century, so why change a proven formula?

The Chinese dependence upon the spoken word was another serious handicap. As every psychologist knows, in Western societies knowledge delivered verbally is poorly retained and is significantly less remembered than the printed word, but it was traditional in Chinese society because the peasantry was illiterate. In Korea the Chinese possessed little written material at first to supplement the lectures of their incompetent political

125

officers. When, ultimately, material printed in the English language was produced, all they could provide in sufficient quantity were newspapers, old copies of *The Shanghai News* or *The Daily Worker*. Unfortunately they misjudged the Westerners' cultural hygiene need for toilet paper. The Commissars were outraged by the use of their precious printed material for this purpose and for rolling cigarettes and there were savage reprisals. Thereafter printed materials, especially their much treasured books were housed in the Chinese headquarters building. Over a period of years stocks of books increased considerably in the camp libraries for issue to a select few progressives.

Over a period of nine months of largely fruitless mass indoctrination there must have been some aspects of Communist philosophy and propaganda with which all the prisoners could agree, just as in British politics a Tory supporter might agree with some aspects of Labour policy without accepting its principles as a whole. Similarly, acceptance of some of the things the indoctrinators propounded did not mean acceptance of Communist philosophy and viewpoints as a whole. What the bulk of the prisoners could not stomach was the compulsion to listen for hours on end and live under a regime which claimed a monopoly of the truth and daily contradicted the assertions of the indocrinators by its own acts of savagery.

However, there were a number of prisoners who took a genuine interest and began forming small study groups, especially in Camp 5. In this camp it was a small number of progressives who approached the Chinese for extra tuition, not the reverse. It must have taken the Chinese a long time to appreciate the advantages of small, voluntary study groups, which in Camp 5 eventually reached a membership of over fifty British prisoners, i.e. twenty-eight percent of the total number of British prisoners in this camp. It might therefore be said that the credit for the success of the Chinese indoctrination programme in Camp 5 was not due to the Chinese but to a handful of progressives prisoners who persuaded their chums to undertake voluntary study, to fill an intellectual vacuum, if not for political motives.

Overall, in Camps 1 & 5 there was a nucleus of about ten per cent of the British p.o.w. who were sufficiently inspired to give their active support to their captors. It has been asserted that these men acted out of self-interest rather than political conviction. This may have been true in the earliest phase of their captivity, prior to the Chinese take-over of the main camps. But subsequently self-interest had to be weighed against ostracism by their companions and the ultimate risk of punishment upon

126

repatriation. It is foolish to suppose that all the earliest progressives made a rational decision to collaborate, although some, such as Comrade and three other former members of organizations affiliated to the Communist Party, may have done so prior to reaching the Yalu River camps. For the majority of the active progressives it is likely that genuine interest resulted in rejection by their peers and made them sitting ducks to Communist blandishments. Among any group of British people there are always some who have a genuine interest in politics and enter into the Trade Union movement or local politics, usually without any kind of formal training in their chosen political philosophy or party political organizations and practices. The Chinese quickly identified these individuals and encouraged them to study. Typical of this was a young private of the Glosters, mentioned several times in Farrar-Hockley's book for his quiet courage in battle. He was a van boy before joining up with low average intelligence and became one of the leading progressives in Camp 1. He brought his notebooks with him when he was repatriated, 300 pages of detailed notes on 173 items of study. They showed that he had cheerfully tackled such formidable subjects as Hegel's and Engels' concepts of Materialism, 19th Century political thought and the materialist conception of world history. Also the history of the British Trade Union Movement, Anglo-Soviet relations since 1918, British, French and German colonialism between 1815 and 1899, with particular reference to the opium wars, the foundations of Leninism, Kalinin's principles of Communism, sociology, economics and anthropology, all, of course, with the Communist bias. He had taken the trouble to compile for himself a dictionary of Communist terms and phases and kept a record of all the books he had read in captivity. This included the works of Dickens, Theodore Dreiser, Stalin and others. Among the more sinister items were descriptions of eight ways of breaking up monopolies by strike action and critiques of strikes at the Park Royal vehicle factory at Acton, strikes at the Silverwood colliery at Rotherham and a strike by railway vanmen in Sheffield.

Clearly the Chinese were bent upon teaching these fledglings more than useless theory. The agitation tactics learned by private tuition were carried into practice in the p.o.w. compounds to raise support of the peace campaigns, petitions and domestic elections. These prisoners, and there were several of them, submitted themselves willingly to private study sessions and returned for more at every opportunity.

In all camps there were two topics of indoctrination that were guaranteed to snatch every prisoner's attention. One was an armistice and repatriation and the other was America's alleged use of germ warfare.

Peace overtures had been initiated by the Russians when the Chinese had driven the U.N. Forces back to the 38th Parallel in May 1951 and called for a cease-fire in June. American and North Korean representatives met for the first time at Kaesong on 26 July. In November an informal cease-fire existed and in December both sides exchanged information on prisoners of war. Then the haggling started, each accusing the other of using the p.o.w. issue as a bargaining chip. The Communists originally claimed that they had captured over 66,000 U.N. p.o.w. but could only produce the names of 11,000. The United Nations held 130,000 North Korean prisoners and 20,000 Chinese, not all of whom wished to be repatriated. And so began the prolonged wrangling over the issue of voluntary or involuntary repatriation which lasted for the next eighteen months with each side blaming the other for the lack of progress.

In the prison camps the prisoners had high hopes of early release when the peace talks started in July '51, hopes that were raised and dashed repeatedly as the haggling continued. Their restraint all but came to an end when, after five months of haggling, the Americans raised the issue of voluntary repatriation. The refusal of over 100,000 Korean and Chinese p.o.w. to be repatriated was a stinging slap in the face for the Communists and speaks volumes for the ultimate ineffectiveness of their close control of the social structure of their troops and their intensive, continuous political re-education programmes. Nevertheless, they coolly accused the United Nations of massive coercion and invoked Articles 7 and 18 of the Geneva Convention. These stated that all prisoners should be repatriated without delay on cessation of hostilities and that under no circumstances can prisoners renounce wholly or in part the rights secured for them under the Convention. This was a classic piece of Communist hypocrisy from nations that were not signatories to the Convention, had refused to recognize it, had vilified it and broken its terms repeatedly in every respect and were now invoking it when it suited them. The Convention itself had been drawn up in a previous era and was never designed to cater for such a contingency as 100,000 p.o.w. refusing to be repatriated.

To many of the British prisoners the stalling of the talks over the issue of repatriation of Orientals was carrying humanitarianism too far. They felt that they were being used as bargaining chips by their own government and it shattered their faith in the sincerity of the U.N. representatives in pressing for a cessation of hostilities and their early release.

The immediate effect was a startling outburst of anti-Americanism in the British prisoners' letters to their relatives and in the broadcasts which the progressives were making over Peking radio and in the Communist press.

The Chinese propagandists had a field day in the prison camps and exploited every twist and turn in the Peace negotiations, blaming every hitch and delay on the Americans. Repatriation was, obviously, a burning issue with all the prisoners and they only had the Communist version of events from which to judge the justice or injustice of the situation for themselves. The stalling did immense damage to their morale.

The germ warfare accusation against the Americans added fuel to the anti-American feelings of the British prisoners. The reasons for the Communists massive international propaganda campaign on the germ warfare issue are obscure. In his official history of the Korean War, General Sir Anthony Farrar-Hockley says it was probably an outbreak of typhus among the North Korean troops in the winter of 1950/51. In Whitehall there were rumours circulating in the Intelligence departments that there was an epidemic of typhus among the Chinese troops returning home from the Korean battlefields. Another rumour said that the Chinese started the accusation as a means of explaining their massive battle casualties to their own population. Whatever the original reason, the Chinese turned it into a major political issue and mounted a world-wide propaganda campaign that successfully convinced many people in the Western world as well as the p.o.w. that America had resorted to the dirtiest of methods to win the war.

It seems that the first accusations came from the North Koreans as early as 1950. In February 1952 Moscow radio accused the Americans of using bacteriological warfare in Korea, presaging a massive interrogation programme by the Chinese on hapless American aircrews to force them to admit to waging germ warfare. The interrogation programme lasted many months as nearly a hundred airmen were mercilessly harried by Chinese interrogators in special centres as far apart as Mukden, the Yalu River camps and Pyongyang. Seventy-eight of these airmen were physically abused and all were starved and subjected to extremes of heat, cold and degradation. Thirty-eight of them ultimately confessed to waging germ warfare but some of these refused to sign their confessions and others retracted them immediately afterwards. Twenty-three of these confessions were used as 'evidence' of the American 'atrocity'.

While the prisoners were being hammered and harried for confessions the Chinese began their propaganda offensive. The foreign language editions of the magazine *People's China* ran a feature article condemning

129

the United States as "an enemy of human justice by committing the monstrous crime of waging large-scale bacteriological warfare". The International Red Cross and the World Health Organization volunteered to send investigators into Korea but were immediately refused permission to enter enemy territory. Instead, the crafty Communists created their own 'International Scientific Commission' made up of their own followers and fellow travellers and invited them to undertake the investigation. Many other Communist 'front' organizations were also mobilized and invited to undertake inspections, including the International Association of Democratic Lawyers. Among them was the Communist lawyer Jack Gasker, who subsequently reported at a press conference in London on 23 April 1952 that the Association had "investigated the atrocities and confirmed the charges".

World-wide, including in the Yalu River prison camps, the Communists mounted special photographic displays of their flimsy, so-called evidence. There were pictures of Koreans wearing face masks supposedly decontaminating their villages, photos of the alleged bombs, of unexploded 'germ' bombs being destroyed by burning them, pictures of the airmen who had confessed to dropping the bombs, and of course full transcripts of their allegedly 'free' confessions.

The tragic part of the whole hoax was that few people in the world, and none of the British p.o.w. in the prison camps on the Yalu River, possessed enough knowledge of the technicalities of biological warfare to discredit the accusations the Communists were making. If such a weapon had been used, there would have been massive loss of life in the regions where the weapons had been supposedly dropped and probably panic among the Chinese p.o.w. camp staff for fear of the diseases spreading. Where was the evidence of massive loss of life or a massive spreading of epidemics? The Communists claimed that every known type of lethal virus had been dropped, anthrax, typhus, typhoid and many others, but there was no evidence of any Korean suffering from any one of them other than typhus, let alone all of them. Moreover, it was claimed that they had been used repeatedly over a long period, disregarding the ludicrous conclusion that the same areas had been re-infected over and over again, without spreading outside the infected zone and with no apparent additional heavy loss of life.

Unhappily, world-wide, a large number of people were taken in by this outrageous hoax and among the p.o.w. even the officer prisoners were left with a sneaking suspicion that the Americans had indeed dropped a few germ bombs.

It is difficult to quantify the effects on the outside world of the propaganda material generated by the prisoners themselves. Their propaganda broadcasts on Peking and Pyongyang radios peaked in November and December 1951, but it is unlikely that the relatives of these prisoners would have been able to tune in to these stations on their radio sets, or, if they did have short wave receivers, they would have been unlikely to have known in advance the times of the broadcasts. There is no knowing what effects they may have made on the rest of the English-speaking world.

The printed material distributed in very large quantities to the English-speaking world was another matter. The earliest booklets, dated 1952, put out by Pyongyang and Peking were printed on very poor quality paper. The first of these, *Our Fight For Peace*, issued through Pyongyang, was a 293-page detailed report on the setting-up of the "U.S. – British War Prisoners Peace Organization" in the Peace Fighters' School, Camp 12, in Pyongyang, and the election of the Central Committee. It is very dull reading, full of protocol and the detailed verbatim statements and political pronouncements of those seeking office. It includes the Minutes of the Informal Meeting of the Central Committee, Speech in Support of the Declaration and Appeal by Corporal X at the 1st General Meeting, Discussion in Support of the Report at the Plenary Meeting "The People of the Entire World are Fighting for Peace Against War" and many similar riveting articles. It is as entertaining as the minutes of a prolonged Local Council meeting by egotistical members of political parties determined to have their say recorded in minute detail and reveals nothing about the nature of the prison camp or the conditions under which the prisoners were living. Nevertheless, it was widely distributed through various international Communist front organizations.

The much more modest but equally poor-quality booklet *Brothers Shall Be*, published in Peking, was far more likely to be avidly read by the relatives of the prisoners to whom, it is believed, copies were sent through the post. It contained numerous articles by British and American prisoners on such topics as Our Life in Camp 3 (which was renumbered Camp 5), No Barbed Wire, Lenient Treatment Policy, and gives the impression of freedom to participate in religious services (an outright lie) and relates the preparations being made for Christmas. It also quoted reports from American and British newspapers, including *The Times*, on remarks about their good treatment given to reporters by prisoners who had been repatriated through the front lines. On 3 May 1951 (at a time when all the British p.o.w. had been appallingly neglected by the North Koreans and were struggling to cope with the Chinese take-over of the prison camps) *The Times* reported a ministerial reply to a Parliamentary Question. It read:–

> Mr Shinwell said that he had no official information but he had read reports from men who had returned to our lines that while in the custody of the Communist Forces they were, on the whole, well treated.

The men who were the source of this information were Privates Fox and Graham of the Glosters, who had escaped from the evacuation columns and others who had been repatriated through the front lines. They had never seen the conditions in many of the transit camps or in the Yalu River prison camps at this time.

Two years later, in 1953, the Chinese issued a glossy picture magazine depicting the happy lives of the prisoners. It was far more professionally produced on good-quality paper and its distribution world-wide must have been very damaging and very convincing in its portrayal of the reasonable circumstances under which the prisoners were being held. Most of the pictures had been taken in Camp 5, in the compounds of the privileged progressives. It included sections on food, health, medical care, competitive sports and recreational activities and preparations for Christmas and photographs of prisoners' letters home. One final item is a letter from the man I have called 'Judas' which reads:–

> Let it be understood by anyone who reads this letter that our cry for peace is not a cry of a trapped man seeking some way out of a P.O.W. camp. Our demand for peace is for the benefit of all mankind. I am the father of three small children. I owe it to them to make my voice heard and do whatever I can to bring peace to this troubled world.

It is tempting to ask if he felt the same after the Chinese had consigned him to a penal camp for his perfidy.

The world-wide nature of Communism reached into every quarter of every country with its official party organizations and newspapers such as *The Daily Worker*, *Ce Soir* and *L'Humanité*, and numerous publications and its myriad of 'front' organizations, such as The International Association of Democratic Lawyers, the British National Assembly of Women and many others. Because of the international connections of these organizations Peking and Moscow could reach into homes and families of every one of the prisoners of war. One of the most sinister aspects of the Korean War was the ability of the interrogators and indoctrinators in the Yalu River prison camps to order the harassment of the relatives of reactionary prisoners and the waverers.

Before the official exchange of the names of prisoners held by the belligerent parties, the only source of information on the identities of British p.o.w. was *The Daily Worker* and the propaganda pamphlets issued by the North Koreans and the Chinese. *The Daily Worker* sent free copies to the relatives of missing men, whose addresses they must have obtained from enemy sources, inviting the relatives to subscribe to the newspaper if they wished for more information about their missing menfolk. The relatives were also sent propaganda booklets and leaflets from Peking, inciting them to demand peace on Communist terms or describing American 'atrocities'.

During the war the Communists had permitted three British fellow-travellers to visit Camp 5. One was a correspondent of *The Daily Worker*, another was Jack Gaster, the left-wing lawyer, and the third was Monica Felton, chairwoman of the Communist front organization, the British National Assembly of Women. They were, of course, only permitted to talk to the leading progressives living in the most privileged compound in the camp and all subsequently returned home to feed the press with colourful stories about how well the prisoners were being looked after.

The relatives of prisoners were also visited by representatives of various Communist 'front' organizations and invited to attend mass meetings demanding an end to the war. Women from Monica Felton's National Assembly of Women visited the wives and mothers of prisoners inviting them to a mass meeting at the Conway Hall in London, offering to pay their expenses, and those who attended this meeting found themselves marching on the House of Commons waving banners bearing such slogans as 'Bring Back our Lads from Korea'. This was at a time when the sons of some of these women were being tortured by their captors and prevented from writing letters home. One woman who had had one son killed in Korea and another taken prisoner was bombarded with leaflets reading, "How many more sons have you got for the millionaire's fighting pool?"

Apart from the callous insensitivity and harassment, these approaches revealed the Communists' ability to apply pressure on the prisoners through their relatives, and their ability to check upon everything the p.o.w. said or wrote in their autobiographies, a very sinister development indeed. There can have been no other war where the enemy, with the power and the means, were free to exert pressure on prisoners' relatives to support an enemy cause, and through the threat of pressurizing relatives to menace the prisoners themselves. There were several cases where prisoners were threatened by their interrogators that their relatives would be harmed if they did not do as they were told.

As we have seen in the previous chapters, the effectiveness of the Communist propaganda on the British p.o.w. varied from camp to camp, with the highest proportion of progressives being concentrated in Camp 5 at Pyoktong to which camp the leading progressives from Camp 1 had been moved for their own safety. There can be little doubt that the prisoners in this camp were made more vulnerable to Chinese blandishments by their prior terrible experiences at the hands of the North Koreans during their evacuation in the winter of 1950/51. After the war there was an extensive enquiry and statistical tests were made confirming this hypothesis and also on many other relevant factors, such as the ages of the progressives and their terms of engagement.

The repatriated prisoners comprised 38% Regulars, 38% Recalled Reservists, 16% National Servicemen and 8% K Volunteers. Many of the Regulars had had their demobilization delayed for the Korean emergency, so that in fact 87% of the repatriated prisoners had exceeded their run-out dates while in captivity. Indeed a considerable number of these men had been due for release just before they went into battle! The average age of the prisoners was about 25 and over 40% of them had previous combat experience. Six of them had been prisoners of war in the Second World War.

Statistical tests revealed that it was the Recalled Reservists who were most vulnerable and disaffected, significantly more so than men on the other types of engagement. Fifteen per cent of them committed major acts of collaboration and twenty per cent minor acts. This compares with twelve per cent and seventeen per cent of the Regulars (many of the 'Regulars' were in fact National Servicemen on extended engagements), and seven per cent and seventeen per cent of the men on short term engagements (National Servicemen on two-year engagements and 'K' volunteers). This finding was scarcely surprising. The Reservists were veterans of the Second World War and had only been out of the Army for five years before being recalled for the Korean War. They had hardly had time to settle down to new careers and raising families before they were recalled to the Colours. It is known that they were very disgruntled on their way out to Korea and it was rumoured that one unit nearly mutinied just before going into battle. Their bitterness on being captured is under-standable. As many of them who became progressives subsequently stated upon repatriation, their primary objective was survival, not allegiance to their country or to the army.

No significant relationship was found between disaffection and the Regiments or units in which they served, with the exception of the Royal Marines. There were eighteen of these and they had the highest propor-tion of progressives among them of any unit.

Overall, 12 per cent of the British prisoners committed major acts of collaboration and 18 per cent minor acts; 63 per cent resisted political co-operation. Eight per cent were active reactionaries. This compares with 15 per cent of the Americans who actively collaborated and 5 per cent who were active resisters. No figures are available of the percentage of American prisoners who committed minor acts of collaboration.

11

CAMP SECURITY & INTERROGATION

Prior to the Korean War the attitudes of our military authorities towards prisoner incarceration was shaped by the prison camp systems used during the First and Second World Wars, what might be called the Stalag mentality. The belligerents had usually consigned newly captured prisoners to cages behind the battlefields where they did little more than establish their identities, ranks, and hopefully their functions before passing them up the line through transit camps to permanent camps in safe areas, hutted camps surrounded by barbed wire, electric fencing and watchtowers, and patrolled day and night by armed guards. In both World Wars there had always been a shortage of manpower for p.o.w. guard and administration duties and consequently second-rate troops or invalids were often used for these purposes. Once in the camps the prisoners were usually allowed to run their own domestic affairs within their compounds, again in order to reduce the number of guards and personnel needed to look after them. In almost every instance there were far more prisoners in the camps than guards.

The size of the camps varied enormously, and obviously the larger the size the more difficult it was for the guards to know what was going on within the camps. The Germans employed snoopers in their camps, some of them English-speaking, guards whom the prisoners called 'ferrets', to make unexpected visits into the prisoners' accommodation and recreation areas in search of contraband and evidence of prohibited activities, including escape preparations.

The more the prisoners are sub-divided the more physical barriers are required and the larger the staff needed to enforce segregation and police their activities. As every prison warder knows, no matter how much the prisoners are sub-divided, however small the sub-groups, when left

136

alone they will always find ways of making mischief. The Russians and the Japanese overcame this problem by working their prisoners to death. The British and the Germans put the OR prisoners to carefully selected types of work, like farming, where they could do the least damage. The officers were not compelled to work, in accordance with the terms of the Geneva Convention, and therefore had the time and opportunity to make mischief.

Another very good reason for sub-dividing prison camps into compounds and sub-groups is to reduce the risk of mass insurrections that could overwhelm the guards.

During the two World Wars it was usual for prisoners deemed to be of intelligence interest to be set aside for interrogation at each stage of their evacuation to permanent camps. They were routed selectively into special enclaves according to the value of the knowledge they were considered likely to possess. They were weeded out for interrogation in a hierarchy of special centres, at the peak of which was a detailed interrogation centre manned by experts in interrogation techniques and knowledgeable in special subjects.

That the Chinese possessed a well-organized system for handling p.o.w. and their interrogation, indeed, unlike the ad hoc arrangements of Western armies, possessed a specialist Prisoner of War Corps with at least six years' experience was as surprising to our military authorities as was their familiarity with the practicalities of controlling group and sub-group behaviour for commonplace security purposes.

Never before in the annals of British military history had an enemy shown such a close interest in the personal affairs of every single prisoner of war as did the Chinese during the Korean War. Their grasp of destructive group dynamics came as a shocking surprise to Western military psychologists and sociologist who had previously regarded the Chinese as a backward third world nation in respect of the behavioural sciences. Certainly the infant science of group dynamics had never been considered as a weapon of war and it had never been associated in Western thinking with prisoner control and interrogation. It transpired that the Chinese interest in this topic had four objectives. The first was the social isolation of individuals to render them vulnerable and prevent friendships growing into conspiracies. (Friendships were forbidden in the People's Army.) The second was to identify potential progressives for political exploitation. The third was the identification of particular individuals for recruitment as informers for counter-intelligence purposes. The fourth was keeping control of large bodies of prisoners.

There can be no better illustration of the value of even elementary knowledge of group dynamics in controlling prisoners than a comparison between the way the Chinese handled U.N. prisoners and the way the Communist prisoners were handled by the U.N. forces in South Korea. What was so remarkable about the Chinese methods was not just their understanding of group, sub-group and inter-personal behaviour, but also the way that they used it to enforce their system of segregation without an army of armed guards or specially constructed physical barriers between compounds and initially without fencing and watchtowers round the camps. Of course they had the insuperable advantage of being in an oriental country where no occidental could hope to pass as a native. They made use of whatever facilities were to hand by siting the camps, requisitioned Korean villages, in remote areas using the natural features of the terrain and the layout of villages and their rural outbuildings to produce a very effective system of segregation and control. They also fed the prisoners upon a debilitating diet that sapped their strength and endurance.

Compare this with the U.N. system in South Korea where over 150,000 Communist military prisoners were held in tented camps, each containing 8,000 men, who were better clothed and fed than their lackadaisical South Korean guards, supported by disinterested American troops with no experience in guarding prisoners of war. The prisoners were divided into fenced compounds of varying size, but averaging 2,000 men, regardless of whether they were Communist zealots or were press-ganged anti-Communists, with 120 men to each tent. The prisoners greatly exceeded their guards in numbers and the camp authorities clearly had no means of monitoring what was going on in the compounds. With so little security and no interference, it is no wonder that the inmates soon organized themselves either into miniature Communist states with all their usual organs for enforcing discipline and political control, or into compounds ruled by Nationalist supporters or gangster cliques. They were also able to trade in contraband with their South Korean and American guards, traffic in messages with North Korean agents outside the camps who were in contact with Pyongyang and import prostitutes who were camped outside the wire in their thousands. In the Communist-controlled compounds the prisoners were able to organize themselves for campaigns of mass disobedience to coincide with the twists and turns of the Peace Talks. Ultimately the unrest exploded into rioting in both North Korean and Chinese compounds where lethal home-made weapons were used, manufactured from metal left on timber supplied to them for firewood. In May 1952 one compound managed to kidnap the American general in

138

charge of the prison camps and held him hostage for several days. It took a large force of American, British and other U.N. troops to restore order by opening fire on the rioters, killing and wounding about two hundred of them. Upon gaining entry into the compounds some were found to possess underground armouries, one had a hospital equipped with implements and dressings stolen from the Americans, and one had an execution chamber where some prisoners had been tried by their own kind in kangaroo courts and killed. Several tunnels were also found running outside the camp to a nearby village where dumps of stolen American weapons were discovered.

The internal control and the rioting in the North Korean compounds had been organized by agents and political commissars led by a North Korean General and his staff. They had infiltrated the camps by the simple ruse of dressing in the uniforms of common soldiers and deliberately surrendering to the U.N. front line forces.

Clearly, if the Communists were capable of organizing insurrections and instituting their own system of control inside the U.N. camps in South Korea they were equally on the alert for agent infiltration and organized resistance in their own camps on the Yalu River. The big difference between the camps North and South of the 38th Parallel was that the Chinese revealed themselves to be surprisingly familiar with the security advantages of splitting the prisoners into small groups, infiltrating every group and setting one small group against another. Moreover, unlike the U.N. forces who were always short of skilled manpower for the front line and short of men for duties in their rear, the Chinese never suffered a shortage of men for any purpose and had plenty of trained men for prison camp duties. The ratio of Chinese to prisoners was at least 1 to 3, supported by ample networks of ferrets and informers, whereas in South Korea the ratio of guards to prisoners was 1 to 125 with virtually no internal control.

The organization of the Chinese system of interrogation of p.o.w., though primitive by Western standards in terms of accommodation and material resources, was based upon classic lines in that they possessed field interrogation teams that set to work on the prisoners soon after capture, although its priorities and targets were substantially different from anything previously experienced by occidental prisoners.

At the outbreak of the Korean War there was, as has already been stated in an earlier chapter, a tendency on the part of British military circles to regard Communist China as yet another satellite state of the Soviet Union which would therefore slavishly copy the Russians in almost all things.

Such a view is untenable after reading the history of Chinese Communism. It was not in the nature of the Mao Tse-tung regime to consider itself inferior or subordinate to any other nation, Communist or otherwise. There were several examples of Chinese officers rebuking Russians in the presence of prisoners of war.

On the whole, though, there was reasonable co-operation between the three Communist countries and varying degrees of co-ordination in military and political matters despite their very different, indeed contradictory, policies regarding the treatment of prisoners of war. There were examples, though few in number, of Chinese troops bullying North Korean soldiers and of Korean military and civilian resentment at the Chinese invasion of their country. But there was clearly co-operation and co-ordination for the political exploitation of prisoners and their propaganda offensives, as is evident from their timing of the creation of the Peace Committees in their respective camps and the launching of their respective germ warfare propaganda campaigns. However, the shabby manner in which the Chinese treated the Peace Fighters of Pyongyang on their arrival in Camp 5 smacks of contempt for their North Korean rivals.

To what extent this co-operation extended to military intelligence is a matter of speculation. The attitudes of the two countries towards their intelligence resources differed dramatically both in their objectives and emphasis. With some notable exceptions, prisoners seized by the North Koreans were treated with typically Russian (and maybe Korean) in-difference to their suffering or their value as individual sources of intelligence. They were regarded as a disposable human commodity exploitable according to the whims of those in charge either for information or for slave labour or both. The North Koreans' haphazard and careless selection and treatment of prisoners for interrogation was in significant contrast to the Chinese who selected their victims with care.

The techniques of interrogation used by the Communists in Korea are a highly emotive subject and have been the subject of a huge amount of comment and speculation by both military and psychological experts. According to many of them it is the other half of the process of Brainwashing. Many of these 'experts' have written books pontificating upon the supposedly scientific behavioural principles underlying the Communists' interrogation techniques. Nevertheless, despite the facts published, for example, by the American Human Resources Research Office, the 'experts' continued to insist, long after the Korean War, on the existence and use of 'scientific' methods of persuasion. Much of what has been written is laughable to anybody who has been a victim or had first-hand knowledge of interrogation systems and how they actually work. One notorious example of ludicrous speculation came from a psychiatrist, allegedly the foremost British expert on Brainwashing, who, in his best-selling book on the subject described its effects thus:–

An intelligent and hitherto mentally stable person who has been brought up for trial behind the Iron Curtain is prevailed upon not only to believe but to proclaim sincerely that all his past actions and ideas are criminally wrong.

In a snide reference to the facts described in the Ministry of Defence Blue Book on the treatment of British p.o.w. in Korea he wrote:-

It seems very difficult to believe that the holding of senior Non-Commissioned or officer rank in the British Army renders one so immune to methods which can result in at least the temporary break-down of a Cardinal Mindszenty.

He tried to make a case for his psychiatric theories of Brainwashing and Thought Control from a sample of about eight cases and made no distinction between the methods used by the Russian-controlled Hungarian secret police in Budapest and those used in the primitive circumstances of Chinese-controlled prison camps in Korea. One wonders if he would have retracted his theories had he taken the trouble to read Krushchev's 1956 report to the 20th Congress of the Central Committee of the Soviet Communist party on how the Secret Police had extracted confessions from their victims. And he probably ignored Cardinal Mindszenty's description upon his release from prison in 1956 (the same year as his book was published) of how the Cardinal was beaten and rehearsed into making his confession of treasonable activities to the Hungarian court. There was absolutely no question of the Cardinal sincerely believing what he had been forced into saying in court.

In almost all of these enquiries and speculations the term 'technique' has been used synonymously with torture and other violent methods of persuasion. Even the highest American military authorities and the medical experts called to give evidence at courts of enquiry into the behaviour of prisoners who had co-operated with the enemy, politically and otherwise, during the Korean War made the same basic assumption. For example the detailed reports of the proceedings at the Court of

Enquiry into how the most senior American aviator captured by the Communists, Colonel F.H. Schwable of the Marine Corps, had been brought to confess to waging germ warfare made the same basic assumption. In addition, this much-publicized enquiry made no distinction between the methods of persuasion used by the Communists on the victims of the sensational 'show' trials in Russia and Eastern Europe, including specifically, the trial of Cardinal Mindszenty in Hungary, and the methods used by the North Koreans in Korea and by the Chinese in Korea and Manchuria. They had all been lumped together and labelled as Communist 'methods' of interrogation, by which they really meant methods of persuasion. It was assumed that the North Koreans and the Chinese were slavishly copying the methods used by the Russians and that all their interrogators applied their methods with a high degree of psychological insight, no matter at what level or under what circumstances they were operating within the interrogation organization!

As will be seen, the assumption that methods of persuasion constitute interrogation 'techniques' is both misleading and wrong. It is an extremely narrow approach that leads only to a dead end, to a catalogue of sickening tortures guaranteed to make most people vomit and lose whatever faith they may have possessed in the alleged intrinsic goodness of human nature. It throws no light upon the real practical aspects of the process of interrogation. By focusing their attention on methods of persuasion in the hope of finding evidence that would justify their assertions of sinister and systematic psychological methods based upon fashionable psychiatric or psychological theories, the Brainwashing experts have merely revealed their profound ignorance of interrogation organizations, of the functions of interrogators at each level within the organization and the history of various methods. In lumping together all methods of persuasion regardless of when they were used, the level at which they were used, the circumstances in which they were used or the facilities available and regardless of the nationalities of the Communist users, the 'experts' revealed that they had never bothered to investigate the work of an interrogation agency, had no inside knowledge of various and genuine techniques of interrogation and revealed an unforgivable lack of discrimination.

The popular idea of an interrogation is that it is a process of overt, confrontational close questioning for information by an identifiable interrogator empowered to punish the victim for failure to respond. (Note the focus on extracting information and no mention of depositing it.) This is a naïve, simplistic and long-outmoded concept. There is no divine edict

142

that impels the interrogator to reveal his identity as such or any compulsion to question the suspect in a blatantly obvious manner or in circumstances indicative of a formal interrogation. Indeed, there is a strong case for arguing that the exclusive use of the confrontational form is the hallmark of the amateur or of a desperate interrogator deprived of the tools of his trade, some of them traditional, like the use of stool pigeons and informers, or deprived of adequate intelligence back-up. As will be seen, the omission of the use of interrogation as a vehicle for depositing information, or, more likely, misinformation, is a serious one.

A victim's perception of direct questioning at an interrogation depends upon the circumstances in which it is carried out. If it is done officiously in formal or threatening circumstances it will obviously be perceived as an interrogation. Effected in a pleasant manner in either formal or informal surroundings it will be described as an interview. But if conducted in a café, or in a bar by an acquaintance or somebody posing as a friend of a friend it may be perceived as an interesting discussion. Yet the same questions may be posed in all three settings. There is an old saw among veteran British p.o.w. interrogators which says why hammer at the bolted and chained front door if there is the option of sneaking round the back!

A systematic job and skills analysis of the work of interrogators reveals some surprising results, including the commonplace use of group dynamics. The author discovered during his own intelligence training, from his conversations with Second World War veterans of M.I.19 who had manned our field and detailed interrogation centres and by doing a systematic job analysis on their work, that our own people were very familiar with it but did not know it by that name. The observation of interpersonal and inter-group relations, i.e. who consorts with whom, was regarded by M.I.19 officers as an elementary, common-sense part the job of controlling p.o.w. and essential for the manipulation of these relationships, e.g. sowing suspicions and breaking up conspiracies and friendships to pre-empt escape attempts, prevent trafficking in prohibited goods and other forms of mischief-making. But of far greater importance to them was that it is vital for the deployment of stealthy interrogation techniques. These sociological factors have rarely been emphasized as an essential element in prisoner control in civil or military prisons and have been ignored, probably because they make exceptionally heavy demands on manpower and resources, especially of trained observers and expensive time-consuming methods of observation. Moreover, these factors have never been recognized as an essential part of an interrogator's skill, partly because the interrogators themselves regarded it as so commonplace that it was scarcely worth mentioning.

The first qualification of an interrogator is mastery of a foreign language in order to detect nuances in the spoken word. In Korea, few of the Chinese interrogators and fewer of the political officers possessed such mastery. They rarely had command of idiomatic English, especially if spoken rapidly, and must have been flummoxed by the regional accents. This is one of the reasons for their continuous, annoying repetition of questions and for their insistence on putting things in writing. The latter is also a substitute for the lack of a good memory and disposes of the need for hours of recording and transcription by mechanical devices or short-hand writers. The Chinese are known to have possessed wire tape recorders and used them for recording the germ warfare confessions of some of the American aviators.

Fundamental to a study of interrogation are two important axioms. The first is that one cannot ask relevant questions unless one is already aware of what is relevant. The second is that it is necessary to know in advance who knows what. When one asks how the interrogator knows what is relevant and whom to question one opens up an enormous field of back-up intelligence techniques and services and an organized system of selective questioning. It is therefore necessary to examine interrogation as a system which includes the extent of its store of previous knowledge, overt and covert methods of information-gathering, including indirect methods like the forensic sciences, clandestine methods such as penetration agents, *agents provocateurs*, stool pigeons, monitoring devices and overt and covert methods of persuasion, as in the film *The Sting*.

The idea that an interrogation is a duel of wits is a nonsense. The victim is pitting his wits against the resources of an intelligence system the base of which is prior collection of knowledge through a process of scanning and search for suitable data and sources. If this does not exist the first job of the intelligence officer is to create what has been called an intelligence environment, setting up a system of surveillance and search procedures such as convincing people that it is their duty to volunteer information. This information produces clues worthy of further investigation which in turn produces further information and so starts a data flow for the compilation of records and dossiers. Some intelligence organizations, especially the MVD, have whole departments devoted to compiling dossiers on a wide variety of individuals (as indeed have many newspapers) prior to their arrest or capture. Once the identities of suitable human or published or communication sources have been established a decision has to be made on the most suitable mode of further investigation or exploitation, that is, overt, indirect or covert techniques. If covert methods are selected they are almost certain to be accompanied by some form of diversion to deflect the victim's attention.

The most obvious technique of interrogation is direct questioning. It is probable that the majority of prisoners of war need very little prodding into answering questions since they are permanently in a life-threatening situation, though much depends upon the nature of the question and the individual's perception of its *military* value. Most men do not put their lives at risk by refusing to answer trivial questions, even if they are of a military nature, and each individual has to judge for himself the threshold point at which he is prepared to accept enemy punishment for declining to answer, and ultimately punishment from his own side if he does. Unless the prisoner is questioned in front of his compatriots, there are usually no witnesses to the questioning or to the value of the information given away, and therefore little risk of him being taken to task by his own side. The skilled interrogator will rapidly determine the individual prisoner's threshold and find ways of pushing him beyond it by overt threats, or, if he is charitable, by using indirect or covert techniques. He will always employ the old trick of airing his knowledge, which may be considerable, to cut away the prisoner's reluctance to speak and often attribute his knowledge to what has already been disclosed by fellow prisoners. By implicating fellow prisoners he also sows the seeds of suspicion, i.e. plants misinformation. Hence the need to observe who consorts with whom. Often the choice of technique depends upon the urgency and value of the information likely to be obtained. Unfortunately, all too many interrogators allow themselves to be stampeded into violence by impatience, lack of training, inexperience or external pressures.

The use of stool pigeons, i.e. secret agents or traitors placed among prisoners, is an ancient method of gaining information and some would say that their recruitment, placement and control is the nub of the interrogator's skill. There are many types of stool pigeon, ranging from a penetration agent, i.e. a trained enemy spy posing as a member of a group, to a genuine member of a group working as a pernicious informer for money or privileges or to escape punishment or execution.

Although stool pigeons can be used almost anywhere regardless of environmental circumstances, there are some covert listening devices, such as hidden microphones, which, in the days of the Korean War, could only be used in special acoustic environments or in static installations. They are most unlikely to have been used in the very primitive living conditions suffered by the majority of British prisoners during their evacuation to the Yalu River camps. The primitive hovels used to house the prisoners in those camps and the 'holes', caves, crevices, woodsheds, barns and cattle pens used to house prisoners under interrogation are also very unlikely places in which to plant microphones. But they could have been used in custom-built prisons such as those used by the North Korean Security Police in Pyongyang and Sinuiju and by the Chinese in their Mukden prison.

In a previous chapter we have seen that the system used by the North Koreans lacked many of the facilities that are fundamental to establishing who knows what. They probably lost most of their military intelligence records during their lightning retreat from Pyongyang, when even the Soviet Legation premises were sacked by the advancing U.N. forces. Also through the previous continuous heavy aerial bombardment of the capital. But it is known that the Korean interpreter attached to one of the British regiments to liaise with the ROK army pioneers who were conveying many of their supplies turned out to be a Lieutenant in the North Korean army! After the British soldiers were captured by the Chinese, the interpreter identified the functions of many of the prisoners. Apart from this one incident, there appears to have been little advanced knowledge of the intelligence value of specific individuals or classes of individuals and no organized system of selecting prisoners for interrogation at Pak's Palace and other interrogation centres. Their appalling indifference to the intelligence value of Sir Vivan Holt and all the other diplomatic prisoners in the early days of their captivity is a good example of North Korean disorganization and amateurism and their lack of discrimination. Batches of military prisoners were drawn indiscriminately from the caves and other feeder camps and the onus of revealing relevant information was placed squarely on the unfortunate prisoners who were frequently beaten up for not volunteering what they knew that might be useful to the enemy. Another indication of their amateurism was their use of interrogators of the rank of Colonel to question prisoners of low intelligence value. Moreover when these interrogators asked for specific information it was often preposterously outside the knowledge that the prisoners were likely to possess, as when junior officer-prisoners were ordered to reveal the plans or coding systems of their high commands or secret services.

In many instances the interrogators lacked sufficient elementary background military knowledge to frame even simple relevant questions and often could not instantly recognize when they were being misled. They relied on handbooks of questions but could not spontaneously evaluate the answers. They seemed to recognize chaff only when somebody behind the scenes, probably Russians, had evaluated the information for them.

As far as is known, only once was an attempt made to plant a stool pigeon among the prisoners in a transit camp, somebody (probably one of the visiting correspondents of a Western Communist newspaper) posing as a British officer who was known by some prisoners to be dead. There is no evidence of the use other methods, including written question-naires, to find out which of the prisoners possessed important military information before subjecting them to interrogation. The North Koreans did not seem to know what they were looking for, and certainly did not relate their interrogation targets to appropriate prisoners at a time when they had an abundance of prisoners to draw from in their transit camps. This is probably the reason for them making a second attack after the pris-oners had reached the Yalu River camps, where the Chinese would certainly have had the time to establish who knew what. But by then it was far too late for useable tactical military intelligence. It is to be noted that the principal target and weight of emphasis of North Korean interro-gations was military and technical information.

By comparison the Chinese were experts and showed a significant understanding not just of the value of creating an intelligence environment from scratch but also of the importance to this objective of imposing a system of small groups to aid their penetration and the identification of individuals for political and intelligence exploitation. By far the most dramatic difference between them and their Allies lay in the priorities, spread and emphasis of their interrogation targets. One post-war survey on repatriated British prisoners indicated that only 5% of the Chinese interrogation effort was devoted to military information, 50% to personal details of the individual and his associates, 35% to investigating reac-tionary plots and browbeating the victims into confessions and 10% into attempting to modify prisoners' political attitudes. Probably the percentage of interrogation effort for military information was much underestimated because few repatriated prisoners would admit to giving away military information for fear of the consequences. Nevertheless, crude though this survey was, it described a very different pattern of interrogation effort from that of the Russian-backed North Koreans.

The Chinese started their search for information soon after they had captured their prisoners. With the Royal Marines captured at Koto-ri they already possessed the means of identifying units and had previous knowledge of the identities of its senior officers, information obtained by their intelligence sources in Malaya.

Among the soldiers it was often easy to identify the prisoners' ranks and functions by the badges sewn on to their uniforms, such as regimental flashes and buttons, parachutes on their shoulders, crossed rifles on their sleeves signifying marksmen and so on. The officers had different colour backings to the pips on their shoulders. (The Chinese never wore any badges of rank or functions on their uniforms.) The enemy are known to have emptied their prisoners' pockets of maps, signals and pay books soon after they had been captured. They were also busy among both the January and April evacuation columns soon after capture, taking some prisoners aside for interrogation while they were still in shock and surrounded by death and destruction, punishing them savagely for failing to answer even trivial questions or for trying to adhere to the Name, Rank and Number policy. The political officers took many prisoners aside for cosy chats about their attitudes towards their officers and fellow prisoners at a time when minor co-operation appeared to provide a means of survival. Many of the prisoners did not regard giving trivial information on their colleagues as military information, nor, they believed, could giving information about themselves be so classified. This applied equally to the information demanded by the spoof 'PW Registration Form' and the abbreviated version of the infamous autobiographical inventories with which some prisoners were provided early in their captivity.

Proof of the Chinese contemporary knowledge of modern sociology and its data-collecting techniques is evident from an examination of any one of several versions of the autobiographical inventories issued to the prisoners during their captivity (see Appendix A). They were re-issued on various occasions and woe betide the prisoner who refused to answer all the questions or whose answers did not tally with his previous answers. They were publicly beaten up as an example to others before being imprisoned and subjected to further punishments, in flagrant violation of their rights to refuse to answer questions under the terms of the Geneva Convention. One version contains thirty-eight questions covering their names, nationality, education and hobbies, their life histories from birth to the time of capture, details of their military histories and their previous jobs, the number of people in their families, their occupations, their possessions, financial circumstances and political affiliations. Questions about the prisoners' military histories and experiences went far beyond their current ranks and functions and included insidious demands to know the names of the man's most intimate friends within his unit and their names and functions. Equally insidious and with far reaching implications in view of the Communists' ability to visit the prisoners' relatives were questions about their names and addresses and their political and religious beliefs. The people named were harassed by unwanted visitors from Communist front organizations and were bombarded with seditious propaganda. Some relatives were threatened into participating in political rallies.

Some of these inventories were undisguised political and social attitude surveys, probing the prisoners' attitudes at being sent to fight in Korea and their attitudes towards their officers. They also probed the prisoners' financial circumstances and those of his relatives and asked what influence these relatives had upon his thoughts and actions. They even enquired into matters that had nothing whatever to do with the war or attitudes, such as the places the prisoners had visited that they liked best and the names of any persons they might have met there!

By our standards the Chinese employed an enormous number of men on p.o.w. camp administration and it is known from Corporal Westwood and others who gained access to their headquarters offices that the data collected from the questionnaires and other sources were carefully recorded in dossiers which the enemy compiled upon every single prisoner.

Much of what the prisoners wrote in their autobiographies could be verified through the enemy's contacts with the British Communist Party, its newspaper *The Daily Worker* and through numerous front organizations. It could also be verified by censoring the prisoners' incoming and outgoing mail. No wonder the prisoners were encouraged to write home! Most of the letters written by the prisoners were never forwarded to the addressees. Several reliable witnesses, ORs as well as officers, including Farrar-Hockley, stumbled across smouldering, partly burned piles of prisoners' mail, both incoming and outgoing, from which extracts had been cut out of the pages before consigning them to the fires.

The issue of informers and informing became the subject of bitter recriminations among the repatriated prisoners as they caused so much suffering. It is extremely difficult to judge its true extent. The British are not used to guarding their tongues in the presence of familiars. Distinctions have to be made between careless talk to compatriots in unguarded moments within earshot of snooping enemy ferrets, lack of due care in plotting and organizing escape attempts or other acts of defiance, reluctantly providing tit-bits of information when sorely pressed and threatened, carelessness under enemy interrogation and wilful pernicious informing at the enemy's bidding. It is known that several escape and resistance groups were 'conspicuously conspiratorial'.

The selection and placement of informers began soon after capture with the appointment of squad leaders to supervise the haphazardly formed squads of about ten men. The earliest squad leaders were often the youngest and most junior members of their squad and they were threatened with being shot if any member of their squad tried to escape or disobeyed orders. After reaching the permanent camps the squad leaders were changed repeatedly and very soon the Chinese-nominated leaders and the squad monitors were recognized by their peers as overt informers. Squad members quickly learned not to exchange confidences in their presence, partly as a tactic to protect the squad leader in the hope that he would not be held accountable for what he honestly did not know. One ranker also pointed out that when in their quarters the squad leader was one man against a dozen others, who could heap retribution upon him in countless mean ways if he was too diligent in the execution of his duties. Consequently the squad leaders were subject to a measure of control by the prisoners themselves, thus limiting their potential as pernicious informers.

The elected representatives of the Daily Life Committees were the interface between the prisoners and the camp staff, and since the committee members did not remain long in office if they declined to co-operate, the incumbents were an obvious conduit of information on the affairs of the prisoners they represented.

The constant re-shuffling of membership of the squads according to their progressiveness or the reverse must have resulted in the progressive squads containing men all reporting on the attitudes of each other, but such a policy denuded the reactionary squads of potential informers. In between were squads comprising prisoners who were trying to minimize their co-operation with their captors. These, and the progressives squads, were easily penetrated by recruiting informers by threats, but the reactionary squads and the squads of British officers were a different proposition. Derek Kinne, G.C., an out and out reactionary, was repeatedly asked to become an informer during his numerous beatings, but always declined to co-operate. And if the enemy tried to recruit him they must also have tried it on others. They are known to have had some success on other known reactionaries, including the one who joined and betrayed Corporal Holdam's escape attempt. In another instance a reactionary prisoner under savage interrogation was forced to sign a contract with his interrogator promising to inform on his colleagues, a document that was used to blackmail him. We know from what happened in the officers' compounds that the Chinese would go to any lengths to break a man into the role of informer, even if it killed him, as when they tortured the American Major T.A. Hume into informing in Camp 5 officers' compound. There is also the example of the American Captain whom the officers had elected as their SUNO. Sometimes they went further and used prisoners as *agents provocateurs*, as they did with Smee in the ORs' compound in Camp 1.

On repatriation all the prisoners were convinced that their squads had been thoroughly penetrated by informers but could name only six men whom they suspected out of over a thousand that were repatriated. But six were not sufficient to have provided coverage for approximately twelve British squads in Camp 5 and thirty-nine in Camp 1 prior to the shake-out of reactionaries. There can be little doubt that the Chinese were very skilful at sowing suspicion and playing off one man or group against another. The true number of pernicious informers will never be known but there were certainly more than six of them among the British p.o.w. Their existence created widespread suspicion and acrimony among all the prisoner groups, officers included, and assisted in the destruction of trust, group loyalties and group cohesion especially among the OR groups lacking leadership.

Overt communications between the informers and their controllers on a regular reporting basis would soon have led to their identification. Consequently they had to adopt less conspicuous methods of communication such as hiding messages in crevices and under rocks, or among their personal possessions to be picked up in snap searches by the guards or by using the outgoing mail boxes as dead letter boxes. All these methods were reported by the prisoners upon repatriation. The informant might also have been arrested for suspected 'conspiracy', along with other members of his squad to provide 'cover', so that he could be de-briefed and re-briefed during interrogation.

There was no known example of the Chinese using a professional stool pigeon, that is, their own trained spy, among the British p.o.w.

It is astonishing that almost all the leading 'experts' on interrogation assume that the victim is the only source of information about himself and his activities, which is patently nonsense. At the trial in America of one of the germ warfare confessors, he pointed out in his defence that the American military authorities had published much information about him in newspapers immediately after he had been shot down! It is fairly obvious that the Communists were monitoring every conceivable overt source of information about individual prisoners, especially their prize victims, senior army officers and aviators. They could easily visit their relatives in the guise of a newspaperman or a representative of one of the many 'front' organizations.

Thus by overt and covert methods did the Chinese compile dossiers on individual prisoners prior to interrogating them.

The means by which the prisoners were forced into compliance, whether by revealing information or participating in some propaganda coup, is the essence of the previous chapters. There is little point in listing all the sadistic methods that were used, be it tying the prisoner's hands behind his back, throwing the running end over a beam and noosing it about his neck, or, as happened to one American officer, throwing him into a slit trench, denying him food or water for eleven days and hammering ceaselessly with rifle butts on a piece of corrugated iron thrown over the top of the trench, driving him to the brink of insanity. The important issue is that it is very unlikely that the interrogators were trained in psychology, nor would it have helped them very much if they had been. They used whatever facilities were at hand, including the weather, to torture the prisoners into doing whatever was demanded.

The idea that the violent methods of persuasion used by the Communists were based upon scientific principles and applied by interrogators who had been formally trained in psychology is nonsense. To assert that these ancient methods were being applied according to some 19th century psychological theory is to read more into the situation and the alleged facts than is justified. Most of the speculators' so-called facts were not facts at all but assumptions based, usually, upon published sources of dubious and often Communist origin. For one thing interrogators work at various levels within their organizations and the lower the level the fewer their resources and the more elementary their training. It is only in urban Detailed Interrogation Centres at the peak of such organizations that they are likely to be manned by the best trained experts armed with extensive resources and unlimited facilities. And even these are usually under the pressures of time and political constraints that precludes the use of time-consuming fancy psychological methods.

The present writer had access to reports on Communist secret police defectors who had been extensively questioned about their interrogation training and could find no suggestion that they had received any training in scientific theories of psychology. They worked by trial and error using techniques handed down by their predecessors since recorded time. Also studied were a considerable number of Russian and East European 'show' trial cases over a period of five years using unpublished intelligence material and there was not a single instance where the prisoner had not been beaten and harried into confessing to a 'crime'. The vast majority of the methods of persuasion employed were traditional, such as sleep deprivation, denial of food and water, solitary confinement and beatings about the body in places that do not show when clothed. Even such elementary methods as compelling victims to sit in the same position for hours or days on end (airlines take note) produces excruciating pain and swelling in the back, hips, legs and feet. All such methods pre-dated both science and Communism. There was not a single instance of the victim 'sincerely believing' what he or she said in open court where they had been thoroughly rehearsed and forced to mouth the Communists' misrepresentation of their deeds.

If there is a real secret of Communist 'Brainwashing' it lies in legal trickery, in the unscrupulous exaggeration of the *actus reus*. Usually the 'illegal acts' to which the victims admitted were of a trivial nature, like smuggling bibles, or small-scale black market racketeering, offences that would not have been elevated to the status of a serious crime, that is, given a heinous interpretation, in any civilized legal system.

Not all the cases sampled by the present writer were so innocent, i.e. comprised trivial acts given heinous interpretation. There were a few cases where the victims had genuinely committed acts that would have been regarded as serious crimes in civilized legal systems, e.g. spying or large-scale corruption of Communist officials. As a general rule, however, show trial victims had been caught red-handed at some act that infringed the Communists' laws, however unjust these seemed by civilized standards, and this was used as a basis for their exploitation for politically highly damaging confessions. In all instances, that is, where the *actus reus* had been real and where trivial acts had been given a heinous interpretation, the victims were not confessing to doing something they had not done, i.e. to a fabricated act implanted in their minds by some mysterious psychological technique. The only exception to this principle was the American airmen who were forced by the Chinese into confessing to waging germ warfare, where the act had not been committed but was fabricated by their interrogators. And in this instance there was absolutely no question of the victims believing that they had committed the act.

The means by which all these unfortunate victims of sensational 'show' trials were brought to confess differed not at all in principle from the ways in which the British p.o.w. were forced into confessing their 'crimes' in the prison camps in Korea. The same old tricks of misrepresentation and

153

heinous interpretation of trivial acts were used. In most cases their alleged 'crimes' would not have been classified as crimes in any civilized society, like the officer charged with 'attempted murder' because in a tussle the rickety door of his cell had fallen off its hinges on to his guard. They were trivial acts which had been given heinous interpretation by a monstrously unjust system and there was absolutely no question of the victims 'sincerely believing' the truth of the misrepresentations of their activities that they were being forced into saying at the bogus trials in so-called 'courts' or in their 'confessions' at public meetings. There was therefore no substance in fact for what the speculators claimed was their 'sincere conversion' to the enemy's interpretations of their deeds.

Thus the bogeyman of 'Brainwashing' turns out to be yet one more outrageous trick of Communist propaganda. At the time, however, it was as terrifying in its hypothetical implication as germ warfare and orbiting hydrogen bombs. How the Chiefs of the Politbureau in the Kremlin and the KGB in their offices in their Lubianka headquarters must have laughed at the panic caused in the highest military and political circles in the West.

12

THE AFTERMATH

On 20 February 1953 General Mark Clark (the American General of World War II fame who had succeeded General Ridgway as C in C of the U.N. Forces) proposed an exchange of sick and wounded prisoners to the Chinese. He must have been very surprised when they readily agreed. On 26 February full armistice talks began, but were accompanied by a flare-up of savage fighting as the Communists attempted to secure advantages in the positioning of the proposed Demilitarized Zone that was to separate North and South Korea. In the midst of these ferocious engagements the parties agreed upon the exchange of sick and wounded prisoners.

On 20 April, at Panmunjon, an unknown number of horrifically wounded Chinese and North Korean p.o.w. were exchanged in Operation Little Switch for 600 sick and wounded U.N. prisoners, twenty-two of them British. One wonders what the Communists did with the grossly disfigured men among their repatriates, since they had shot all their badly wounded soldiers and prisoners of war on the battlefields because they did not possess the medical facilities necessary to cope with them.

The British authorities at Panmunjon rapidly became aware that a number of their repatriates were neither sick nor wounded, but were progressives from Camp 5 whom the enemy could rely upon to feed the Western press with colourful stories about how well they had been treated in captivity. They were all flown to the RAF base at Lyneham in Wiltshire and by the time they landed the British press was already reporting that they had been heavily indoctrinated by the Communists and stated that "specially trained officers had arrived to re-educate them".

The press had evidently picked up rumours that were flying around Whitehall about how the repatriates should be received, whether or not they should be subjected to counter-indoctrination, and if so by whom. In A.I.9, the Prisoner of War Intelligence agency, there was some discussion about the counter-indoctrination proposal and suggestions were made about giving the task to the Army's Education Corps. As the resident psychologist I pointed out that we possessed no propaganda organization that could possibly match the Communists' and that, anyway, 87% of the repatriates were overdue for demobilization and neither they nor their relatives would thank the authorities if they delayed their demobilization for political purposes.

Eventually word came down from the Cabinet Office that no attempt would be made to retain and counter-indoctrinate the repatriates, which left another difficult decision to be made by the War Office. What was to be done about the progressives, especially those who had acted as informers or had otherwise misbehaved themselves in captivity?

The Little Switch repatriates were taken to Tidworth Military Hospital for thorough medical examinations and were placed in beds in a ward which had been set aside for their exclusive use. It was there that a team of officers from the Intelligence Corps, and myself, were sent to interview them in depth. As I was the only civilian in the party I was provided with the uniform of a Lieutenant in the Army Dental Corps to avoid awkward questions from the awaiting pressmen hanging about outside the hospital. In view of the counter-indoctrination rumours that were flying about it was easy to imagine the meal they would have made had they discovered that I was a psychologist and the official expert on Brainwashing. Indeed, some weeks later, in civvies, I visited some of the patients who had been transferred to the Royal Herbert Military Hospital in Woolwich and had scarcely passed through the gates when I was preceded on the grapevine by the rumour that I was "the man from M.I.5"! I played on it for all I was worth while interviewing one scallywag.

We soon discovered that, although all of the repatriates were undernourished and were still suffering from the insanitary conditions in which they had been kept for years, about a third of them did not qualify as seriously sick or wounded, but had been released simply to praise their captors. We discovered that a considerable number of genuinely very ill and wounded British prisoners had not been repatriated. In other words, the Communists had done the dirty on us yet again for their own political advantage.

The Korean Armistice was signed on 27 July 1953. According to its terms all prisoners were to be repatriated within sixty days except for those who had elected to remain behind who were to be placed into the care of the Neutral Nations Commission. There was only one British prisoner in this category, Marine Andrew Condron. And so began Operation

Big Switch during which 75,000 Chinese and North Koreans were swapped for 12,773 U.N prisoners of war.

Altogether about 955 British prisoners were released in small batches at Panmunjon and received a tremendous welcome from the receiving American and British representatives. As the names of those released filtered through to London the lists were searched for the names of the reactionaries who had been consigned to punishment camps and fears grew that some of them would be retained to serve out the sentences so recently passed upon them for their alleged 'crimes'.

Some of our fears of Chinese duplicity were justified. They had admitted Red Cross representatives into North Korea but had tricked them into leaving before they could interview any prisoners. The officers at Pin Chon-Ni were not released from their camp until 19 August. Just before their departure they were joined by Colonel Carne who had just been released from nineteen months of solitary confinement. They were taken to a railhead at Manpo-Jin where they saw Major Sam Weller and other prisoners from the penal camps being put aboard the train under guard. From there they travelled to Pyoktong and thence via Pyongyang to Kaesong station, to a nearby tented camp. They were held there for eight days, before repatriation began, the food and conditions deteriorating daily. They wondered if any of them would in fact be released or whether, once again, they were being deceived and cheated. Colonel Carne disappeared one afternoon, leaving his fellow officers wondering if he was going to be held back, but he returned after a brief period to report that he had been taken to a camp containing British NCOs for an interview with the detested Wilfred Burchett, the correspondent of the Communist newspaper *Humanité*. Burchett had been greeted by the sergeants with boos of derision as he entered their camp and he failed to get a story from his interview with the Colonel, who, when asked how he had been treated, gave him short shrift. At last the officers and ORs were repatriated in small batches.

The ORs from the two main penal camps at Song-ni and Changsong told a similar story of delays, frustrations and fears of being held back. They were eventually taken to the main repatriation camp and released in dribbles among the others from the main camps.

Among the very last prisoners to be released were Sam Weller, Tony Farrar-Hockley and Derek Kinne, none of whom were aware of our fears for their safety that the delay in their release had caused us.

All the repatriates were taken to Japan for medical examinations and initial debriefing. They were eventually embarked in troopships and moved to Hong Kong. The treacherous Smee who had betrayed escape attempts in Camp 1 was tossed overboard by his compatriots both in Japan and in Hong Kong Harbour and had to be removed and sent home in a oil tanker. Various other progressives were beaten up and one or two dumped overboard. The main body of repatriates arrived in Southampton on 14 October, to be greeted by the Duke of Gloucester and other dignitaries.

Of immediate concern to the Intelligence authorities was whether the Communists had swapped any of our men for some of theirs and how many of ours may have been 'turned' or blackmailed into spying for their former captors. As the vast majority of the repatriates were overdue for demobilization it narrowed the field dramatically to a small number of officers and ORs on long-term engagements. The most suspect element was the Royal Marines which had the highest proportion of progressives among their eighteen repatriates.

After these marines had completed their leave Major Cyril Hay of the Intelligence Corps and myself spent a week at the Royal Marines barracks at Eastney, Portsmouth, questioning them in depth. Two of them had been, with Condron, among the 'Inner Wheel' of progressives running the affairs of prisoners in Camp 5. After days of close questioning the Marine being questioned, apparently very sympathetically by Cyril Hay, disappeared overnight. After an intensive search of the barracks he was eventually found late the following morning locked in a lavatory where he had spent the previous evening and the night racked by doubts that the crafty Major had sown in his mind about the validity of Communist assertions, how much allegiance he owed to the Party after the inhuman treatment he had received and about how much information he should reveal to us. Cyril Hay took his prey for a long walk in the country and when they returned he had obtained everything we wished to know about what this pair had been up to in captivity and since their release.

They had agreed to maintain contact with Andrew Condron and during their leave they had visited the British Communist Party's London headquarters in King Street, Covent Garden, where they had intended to confirm their allegiance and seek guidance on how best they could continue to serve the cause. To their surprise and disgust they were given an angry reception and were told to go away. These were the days when there was an enforceable law of sedition, when there were severe penalties for trying to politically corrupt members of the armed forces. They next visited meetings of the Communist Party in their home towns and were not impressed by the locals' lack of familiarity with Party principles and procedures or with the calibre and personalities of those in charge. The two Marines were bitterly disillusioned. They had enjoyed considerable power and influence in captivity; now they were being treated as lepers and nonentities.

When we had completed our investigations at Eastney we were left with the uneasy suspicion that in addition to our prime suspects, one or two more of them had not entirely severed their contacts with their erstwhile hosts, albeit through 'front' organizations. We passed our suspicions on to the Security Service.

It is not known what became of these former p.o.w., but it would have been surprising if they had been compelled to honour their long-term contracts of engagement. After all, what unit commander would want avowed Communists in his ranks at the height of the Cold War? Suspicion, however unjustified, would probably also blight the prospects of all the Marines who had been in captivity. Indeed, events were to show that our suspicions of the Marines presaged far greater fears that were to grow and haunt the Government and military authorities during the next decade about the loyalty of anybody who had been a prisoner of the Communists, especially after discovering in 1961 that George Blake had been recruited as a spy while in captivity. That case led to the setting up of the Radcliffe Tribunal to review the issue of security in the public services and to consider whether limits should be placed on the promotion prospects of anybody who had been detained by the Communists.

No decisions were taken on what should be done with Marine Andrew Condron, who had refused repatriation, should he return to this country at some future date. He was a much-wanted man to answer for his collaboration and many allegations of perfidy. He spent about a decade in China before returning to this country. No legal action was ever taken against him, setting what must be regarded as a very bad precedent.

It took the staff of A.I.9 the better part of two years to complete the detailed debriefing of all the repatriates, collate the reports, extract the lessons to be drawn therefrom and supply evidence to the numerous special committees set up by the Government and the War Office to study various questions arising from the Communists' mistreatment of their prisoners.

Investigation of the many allegations of informing and aiding the enemy were handed over to the Military Police. Several of the repatriates, including Corporal Westwood, had smuggled out of captivity documents which they believed would provide proof for the purposes of prosecution, but it seems that these were not regarded as legally acceptable evidence.

Wisely perhaps, our military authorities, unlike the Americans, did not launch a wave of premature prosecutions against collaborators, most of whom in our case were Recalled Reservists overdue for demobilization. It is easy to imagine the political uproar that would have ensued from their further retention while their prosecutions were being prepared. There were no cases of British personnel behaving like the Americans who had robbed their dead comrades, turned the very sick out into the cold to die and otherwise exploited the helpless for personal gain. As no British personnel were involved in the germ warfare hoax, there were no Courts of Enquiry similar to the February 1954 trial of Colonel F.H. Schwable into the culpability of prisoners making politically damaging confessions.

The Chinese had revealed the limitations of the Name, Rank and Number policy which had its origins in the terms of the Geneva Convention. A ruthless enemy simply did not accept it and easily compelled prisoners to say much more by using a degree of physical abuse out of all proportion to the value or significance of the information demanded.

In the midst of the trial of Colonel F.H. Schwable the American weekly newspaper, the *Army-Navy-Air Force Register* wrote:–

> It is now quite clear that American defence forces must move quickly to formulate POW policy guidance far more adequate than the Geneva Convention. . . .
> The Name Rank and Serial Number do not now suffice. The question facing American defence forces much more concerns what can be revealed other than the Geneva provisions. Military and naval witnesses in the Schwable case demonstrated that they had nothing to fall back on except individual judgement in yielding to or withholding from the enemy information beyond name, rank and serial number.

The paper went on to demand that the Marine Corps set up a task unit to come up with a means of meeting the existing hazard.

The germ warfare confessions raised the question of how much significance our military authorities should attach to the alleged damage caused by widely publicized 'confessions' which in retrospect turn out to have been forced out of unfortunate prisoners. My own recruitment into A.I.9 was but one indication of the seriousness which our own military authorities attached to confessions, politically damaging statements made by individuals and to political rallies, all of which, in the event, turned out

160

to lack any kind of genuine changes of political sympathies on the part of the prisoners. The official view was that they were not only politically damaging to the Allies cause (which is what our enemies hoped we would think), but signs of cowardice and treachery in the eyes of the military authorities. It is obvious that they should not have given rise to outrage on the assumption that they were evidence of political defection and treachery. The odds were heavily in favour of them being the products of coercion. In future the military attitude should be the reverse. It should be assumed that such statements have been made under duress until there is reliable evidence to the contrary. If this was made official policy and widely promulgated as such to the media and to our troops, it would do much to kill the value of the enemy's political exploitation of prisoners and relieve our men of a considerable amount of stress when under interrogation or enemy pressure to participate in political activities on the enemy's behalf.

In this country an investigation into Conduct After Capture was carried out by a committee (of which I was a member) set up by the War Office under its Director of Personal Services, Major-General C.E.A. Firth. It was clear that the Geneva Convention in respect of p.o.w. was being ignored by Communist belligerents and indeed had not been ratified by the United States. It had been ignored by our enemies during the Second World War, during which Italy was second only to Japan in its ill-treatment of British p.o.w. It seemed that Britain was the only signatory to have more or less observed its terms during the past half-century. Read with detachment, some of its terms are archaic and belong to a previous century. For example, it says that prisoners should be given deference in accordance with their rank and age and allowed to keep badges of nationality and rank. If required to work they must be paid a fair rate and working conditions must be reasonable. Officers are not obliged to work. Question: Is the rate for the job to be judged by the prisoners' standards or by the standards of the detaining power? The Chinese did not pay their own troops and even if they did the rate would have been derisory by any Western standards. Another example is that the detaining power must provide prisoners with quarters as good as those of their own troops. Question: What if their own troops are billeted in the hovels of local oriental peasants without sanitation? The same question might also be raised over the quantity and quality of food.

Since the Korean War most of our enemies, including the former Yugoslavs, have treated p.o.w. abominably and have not subscribed to the terms of the Geneva Convention. This being the case, it would seem reasonable to suggest that our whole approach to Conduct After Capture should be reviewed.

The Firth Committee was informed by the A.I.9 representatives that officers of its executive organization in Korea, I.S.9, had been rebuffed by many British commanding officers of front-line units who took the view that their troops were there to fight to the last round and the last man; they were not going to have their men demoralized by instructions on what to do if they were captured! As a consequence when disaster struck these troops were stunned into immobility, made no attempt to evade capture and had little if any knowledge of living off the land and survival techniques. Many of them had thrown away their mess tins and cutlery to lighten their burdens during their long march to the Yalu River, actions they were bitterly to regret when food did eventually become available and they had nothing to put it in.

Whether or not the Services modified their Name, Rank and Number policy or took any notice of the Firth Committee recommendations is not known, but from recent conversations with senior army officers it seems that, if they did, the changes have not been widely promulgated.

At that time, the mid-1950s, only special service troops and aircrews were given escape and evasion training and experience in living off the land. The difference between escape and evasion is that escape occurs after capture and evasion means avoiding capture. It seemed that the whole concept of escape and escape lines was outdated. Our present and future enemies were likely to be culturally and ethnically different, with hostile populations who would not be likely to aid foreigners on the run. It was obvious from the Korean experience that escaping could be made impossible. But evasion was not, as was evident from the operations of our special forces behind Communist lines.

Whether or not our military authorities will expand training in evasion to all troops is a matter of speculation. It is not possible to prepare fighting men for the shock of capture that usually numbs men into immobility at a time when they need to keep their wits about them if they are to evade successfully. Most troops these days are trained to wriggle about the landscape unnoticed, making expert use of the terrain, so that the most urgent need is for them to be taught survival techniques, i.e. how to live off the land, and above all how to find and purify water.

In Korea the helicopter and the notion of snatch pick-ups were in their infancy; the full potential of helicopters had not yet been realized and in any case they could not yet fly at night. But experiments had been carried out using Dakota aircraft trailing a wire to snatch an individual off the ground; it proved to be too dangerous. However, the idea of snatch pick-up was born and was to develop in feasibility as helicopter capabilities improved. In conjunction with homing devices the snatch pick-up has become a reality and was used with great success during the Gulf War and in the wars in the former Yugoslavia for rescuing special forces personnel and aircrews.

The downfall of Russian Communism has not been followed by a revolution in China which remains wedded to their version of Communism, has a massive standing army and can no longer be regarded as a third world nation in the fields of technology and science. North Korea remains not only a Communist nation, albeit its own version of that brand of politics; it is also an unpredictable rogue state that treats its own people abominably. World wide, dictatorships and war lords abound and it seems very unlikely that these will pay any heed to the pleas of United Nations politicians for the humane treatment of prisoners of war.

Tailpiece

British soldier P.O.W. in a letter to his parents.	Tell the family that we are being well fed and well treated. Don't forget to tell this to all my pals in the Dog and Duck and most of all don't forget to tell it to the Marines.
British Officer P.O.W.	Beware of anybody who claims a monopoly of the truth.
Chinese Officer P.O.W	The Communists have no truth. Only that which serves the current party line is the truth.
Chinese Officer P.O.W.	The Communists create people who cheat the people, and the people in turn learn how to cheat them.

APPENDIX A

AN OUTLINE OF AUTOBIOGRAPHY
(CHINESE P.O.W. QUESTIONNAIRE)

This is one of many versions of the autobiographical inventories issued by the Chinese to British p.o.w. in Korea. Its command of our language and the sophistication of its questions is surprising, indeed so much so as to suggest that it was produced by, or with the help of, a British citizen. Many of the expressions used are British, as distinct from American e.g. the use in Section 4B of the word 'colleagues' instead of 'buddies'.

This version is of unknown date. Rumour had it that some of the progressives in Camp 5 were assisting the Chinese to improve their written English in the same way that the Peacefighters of Pyongyang were used by the North Koreans to re-write their propaganda materials.

1. Brief description of yourself.

    1 Names, serial number, rank, age, outfit and duty
    2 Nationality, race and origin, native town and present address
    3 Education
    4 Specialities
    5 Hobbies

2. Family self and parents' financial condition.

    1 Members of family, names, occupations, political affiliations and religious beliefs
    2 Stock and property
    3 Principal source of family income, monthly income, expenditure and savings
    4 Financial tie between you and your parents or wife
    5 Attachments with your parents while you were in the armed forces
    6 Parents' address

3. Social Relationships.

   1 Names and present address of your closest relatives and friends
   2 Their occupations, religious beliefs and political affiliations
   3 Degree of relationship between you and them

4. History in detail.

   A. Before joining forces

   1 Birthday and birthplace
   2 School life, schools you attended, when and where
   3 Professional life, your jobs and pay
   4 Your political activities and party affiliations both during and after schooldays

   B. Military career.

   1 When, where, why and how did you enter the armed forces
   2 Assignments (times, places, units, rank, duties and principal functions)
   3 Your intimate colleagues (officers and men) in the past various assignments
   4 What kind of military training have you received (when, where and in which units) The main courses and subjects studied
   5 How many times have you entered the armed forces
   6 Have you ever been discharged. If so list civilian jobs and pay
   7 Did you fight in World War II If so where and what were your duties
   8 Were you wounded or captured during World War II
   9 How many campaigns have you participated in, when and where

5. Social activities and political affiliations.

   1 What party social bodies and religious groups have you joined (time, place, where and when)
   2 When did you work for them, what were your functions and activities in the organization
   3 The training and education you received from the organizations which you joined
   4 What is the nature and purpose of the organizations you have joined
   5 When were the organizations founded and who were their leaders
   6 Have you kept contact with the organization (prior to and after capture)

7 What are the activities of the parties, organizations and religion you belong to in the armed forces. Are these activities legal or not

8 What is your impression towards various political parties and social bodies in your country

6. Prior to and since capture.

1 Your sentiments and feelings at being sent to Korea, after getting into combat and since capture

2 Impressions of the Chinese People's Volunteers

3 Time and place of capture

INDEX